Rate Yourself on Romance

Rate Yourself on Romance

The Editors of RateYourself.com

A PERIGEE BOOK

A Perigee Book
Published by The Berkley Publishing Group
A division of Penguin Putnam Inc.
375 Hudson Street
New York, New York 10014

Copyright © 2002 by Rate Yourself LLC
Text design by Tiffany Kukec
Cover design by Ben Gibson
Cover illustration by Artville by Eyewire

First edition: August 2002

Visit our website at www.penguinputnam.com

Library of Congress Cataloging-in-Publication Data

Rate yourself on romance / by the editors of Rateyourself.com.
      p. cm.
   ISBN 0-399-52791-5
      1. Dating (Social customs)—Miscellanea.   2. Man-woman relationships—
Miscellanea.   3. Love—Miscellanea.   4. Personality tests.   5. Self-evaluation.
I. Rateyourself.com

HQ801 .R2585 2002
306.7—dc21

2001055160

Printed in the United States of America

10   9   8   7   6   5   4   3   2   1

CONTENTS

Compatibility   91

Working to Make Love Work   133

Introduction

ongratulations. You're reading these words, so you've decided to challenge yourself on the love meter. You have indicated a desire to ask yourself questions that will lead you down a path toward self-knowledge, if not self-love. Now it's your job to listen to what you have to say to yourself by the answers you give to the questions in this book. And to see the picture that your answers paint by the results generated by each survey. Then, when you've finished taking these surveys and learned a bit more about yourself, make the necessary attitude adjustments to help you live a more love-filled life. We all know that living life happily is an endless series of adjustments.

Among the greatest challenges on the path to learning and growing is the ability to ask yourself the hard questions. The psychologists and counselors at your disposal through these pages have done that for you. The surveys included here feature some of the same questions they ask their clients in one-on-one or group sessions, as well as questions crafted especially for these evaluations, crafted to get the most honest self-assessment from people taking these surveys privately. The questions are in your hands. Answering them is your responsibility. It's up to you to be straightforward and honest in response to their probing. Previous survey takers have commented that they feel comfortable being honest when taking these surveys because they can do so privately. None of our professionals will be in the room listening to your answers, so you can be completely open with yourself when answering the questions they have put together.

Pay attention not only to the final assessment that your responses add up to, but also think about the individual questions being asked, and how you answer them. Most of the situations represented by the questions here will be familiar to you, but it is unlikely that you have challenged yourself with your decision in the face of these questions. Face these challenges here—privately—and gain experience for the "real world," beyond these pages. Our previous survey takers have told us about their newfound self-assurance when a question originally presented to them in these surveys surfaces in their lives, and they face it with assertiveness and experience. Enjoy the process of answering the questions, not just the learning from the results.

In addition to taking the surveys alone as a form of self-discovery, this process can be shared with other people. Whether you choose to take the surveys with a romantic partner or a close friend who understands your relationship behavior, sharing the tests can be fun and informative. There is a lot to be gained by allowing others to see and understand your answers, and the surveys can open up wonderful discussions and interactions. Couples use the survey as a novel way to get to know one another by trying to see if they can predict each other's choices and learn about each other by understanding their answer selection.

In this collection of forty self-assessment surveys you'll find a range of topics from marriage to compatibility to sexual creativity. Whether you use this book to help you take an objective look at your current romance or whether it's just for fun is up to you.

Notes on Taking the Surveys

The surveys in this book have been designed to be taken in their entirety before scoring your results. No cheating! To get the truest sense of how you rate, we suggest that you keep a pen or pencil and a scrap of paper handy. Write down the question number and the letter of the answer you chose for each question. Then, when you are finished with all of the questions in a survey, turn to the scoring section and see how you did.

Our team of psychologists and counselors are pretty good at figuring out when clients in their offices are telling untruths. They're not good at doing that with people reading this book. Be completely honest and open with yourself, and get into the flow of the survey without considering how you will score. Remember, you are the only one seeing your evaluations here, so be honest with yourself. . . .

Dating and Relating

Even those of us who consider ourselves relationship experts admit that meeting the right person in today's busy world is a tremendous challenge. Flirting can be fun, but when you're looking for love, meeting new people and making first impressions can try your patience and test your soul.

It's often hard to know if you're sending the right signals to your date and it can be equally difficult to judge the messages that your date is sending you. The surveys in this section will help you understand if your dating strategies are working and what you can do to make them more effective. Although the dating world isn't always easy, try to enjoy yourself. It may take a few tries before you meet the right person, but keep a positive attitude and you're likely to have fun and meet interesting people along the way.

Do You Know How to Meet Single People?

1. Where would you most likely hang out if you were trying to get a date?

    a. A noisy bar or disco

    b. The Laundromat on a Sunday afternoon

    c. Outside of a center for couples therapy

    d. A coffee shop in a hip neighborhood

    e. An amusement park on a family-themed weekend

2. What do you usually do on Friday nights?

    a. Make dinner for myself and watch some television or a video

    b. Meet a few close friends for dinner or drinks

    c. Gather with a group—some old friends, some new

    d. Carefully recompose, but never submit, my singles ad

    e. Hit happy hour on the downtown scene

3. You meet an attractive person you might be interested in. Do you check for a wedding ring?

    a. Instantly

    b. Only if I'm considering asking them out

    c. Sometimes

    d. Never

4. It's been said that you should never leave the house without looking your best, because you never know when you might meet someone. Do you agree or disagree?

   a. Strongly agree

   b. Agree, but with reservations

   c. It would depend on where I was going

   d. Strongly disagree

5. What's the first question that you'd ask a good friend who had a new love?

   a. How they had met

   b. If the new love has any cute friends

   c. How your friend knew this was "the one"

   d. If this would mean that your friend would no longer be available for you

6. Do you ever make eye contact with strangers in public places?

   a. All the time

   b. When I'm feeling adventurous

   c. Never

   d. Only if I notice someone who seems especially intriguing

7. Have you ever given a stranger your telephone number?

   a. Never—and I never would

   b. I give out my number as often as I can

   c. No—but if I had a good feeling about someone, I might

   d. Just a few times

8. Which of the following do you consider to be a great opening line?

    a. "Hey, baby, what's your sign?"

    b. "Ummm . . ."

    c. "Can I buy you a drink?"

    d. "You look very familiar, have we met before?"

    e. "I don't mean to intrude, but I noticed that you're reading . . ."

9. A friend asks you to join a book group for singles; you only know one or two other members. What would you do?

    a. I'd join, but I wouldn't say much the first few times

    b. I would refuse, and suggest that my friend and I just meet for coffee and talk about books

    c. I'd join, but only attend intermittently

    d. I'd join instantly, and send all the other members my vital stats over email

10. A wedding is . . .

    a. A romantic backdrop and a place to meet new people

    b. A chance to connect with old friends and meet new ones

    c. Something that I'm sure I'll never be part of

    d. A grim reminder of my single state

11. Have you ever thrown a party? If so, what kind?

    a. A huge bash for everyone I knew, friends and friends of friends

    b. An intimate dinner for close friends

c. An elegant affair where some people came alone and some brought dates

d. I've never thrown a party—I'm too busy going out to entertain

e. I've never thrown a party—I consider myself fairly antisocial

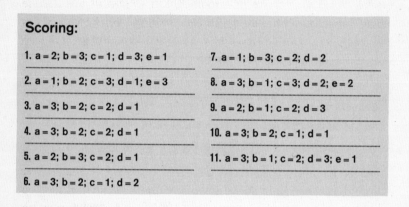

Scoring:

1. a = 2; b = 3; c = 1; d = 3; e = 1

2. a = 1; b = 2; c = 3; d = 1; e = 3

3. a = 3; b = 2; c = 2; d = 1

4. a = 3; b = 2; c = 2; d = 1

5. a = 2; b = 3; c = 2; d = 1

6. a = 3; b = 2; c = 1; d = 2

7. a = 1; b = 3; c = 2; d = 2

8. a = 3; b = 1; c = 3; d = 2; e = 2

9. a = 2; b = 1; c = 2; d = 3

10. a = 3; b = 2; c = 1; d = 1

11. a = 3; b = 1; c = 2; d = 3; e = 1

• What Your Score Means

11 to 17:

Stubbornly Single

Clearly, you're the kind of person who prefers the company of a select few to the splendor of the masses. While it's great to be comfortable with being alone, it might be time to reconsider whether, by refusing to come out of your shell, you're inadvertently narrowing your own horizons. Meeting new people is difficult, but it's a challenge that is often its own reward—even if you don't make any dates, you'll often expand your view of the world by taking a chance on someone new. Push yourself—you could be surprised by what you discover!

18 to 26:
Open to Possibilities

You're confident and comfortable with your single status, so you don't feel the need to constantly be looking for new contacts. This confidence is a great draw to other people—when you *do* feel motivated to talk to someone new, it's clear that that person is pretty special. Whether you are in a room full of singles or a few close old friends, you are open, warm and inviting, and these qualities will bring you more potential partners than a thousand good pickup lines. So relax, and enjoy yourself!

27 to 33:
Patrolling the Market

Your single-people-meeting skills are finely honed. When it comes to looking for potential partners, the world is your oyster and every situation and social event is a possible place where you could cross paths with a new suitor. While it's always great to remain open to the possibility of meeting new people, you should be careful to consider the feelings of your old friends—you don't want any of them to feel like their friendship is less important than finding a romantic partner. When push comes to shove, old friends are more important than new blood. Still, you've got a great attitude toward meeting new people, and you could probably give lessons in how to get a date!

What Kind of First Impression Do You Make?

1. At any given time, you have on hand:

   a. Gum or breath mints

   b. Nothing

   c. Gum, comb or brush and perfume or cologne

   d. Your business card to give to new people

2. When you meet a romantic prospect for the first time, do you:

   a. Shake hands and introduce yourself

   b. Fold your arms and nod your head

   c. Give them a warm hello or a kiss on the cheek if it's a social setting

   d. Always repeat the new name so you remember it

3. In preparation for a blind date, you:

   a. Select a nice outfit

   b. Go straight from the gym, but remove all signs of sweat

   c. Consult all your friends for wardrobe advice and get a new haircut

   d. Nothing—no need to prepare

4. You're going to dinner at your significant other's parents' house for the first time. You would probably:

   a. Try to be relaxed and enjoy the meal

b. Be friendly and polite the entire evening

c. Send flowers (or some other gift) ahead of time and/or bring a gift that night

d. Show up with some fresh flowers or a bottle of wine and a smile

5. You've got an interview for a job you really want. You are most likely to:

a. Do your best to impress the interviewer with your skills and experience

b. Send the interviewer a pair of tickets to a sporting event, as a thank-you after the interview

c. Buy a new suit, put on a good show and send a thank-you note

d. Research the company and industry in advance to make it clear that you're interested and informed

6. If people were to talk about the first time they met you, they'd remember:

a. Your smile and pleasant conversation

b. How great you were to them, getting them drinks and giving rides home

c. That you seemed like a nice person

d. Nothing in particular

7. The music at the party makes you want to dance. You:

a. Rush to the middle of the dance floor and try all of your best moves to impress onlookers

b. Move to the dance floor and mingle with the group

c. Don't want people to see you dance because you're self-conscious

d. Hop out on the dance floor, pushing folks out of the way if necessary

8. You start your new job tomorrow. You are most likely to:

    a. Lay out your brand-new suit and set two alarm clocks an hour earlier than usual so that you know you won't be late

    b. Arrange to have flowers delivered to yourself on your first day of work

    c. Follow your usual work routine

    d. Plan a nice outfit to wear for your first day and set your alarm fifteen minutes early to give yourself some extra time

9. You're new to the neighborhood. You would probably:

    a. Lie low and hope no one recognizes that there is a new face around

    b. Have a big barbeque for your new neighbors to introduce yourself

    c. Join some local organizations so you can meet new people

    d. Greet your neighbors with a wave and smile when you see them out and about

10. During a walk through the park, you're greeted by the dog of a passerby. You:

    a. Say, "Nice dog," or simply smile

    b. Ignore them

c. Ask the owner to control the pooch

d. Rave about what a nice dog and then compliment the owner, too

Scoring:

1. a = 2; b = 1; c = 3; d = 2

2. a = 2; b = 1; c = 3; d = 2

3. a = 2; b = 1; c = 3; d = 1

4. a = 1; b = 2; c = 3; d = 3

5. a = 1; b = 3; c = 3; d = 2

6. a = 3; b = 3; c = 2; d = 1

7. a = 3; b = 2; c = 1; d = 3

8. a = 3; b = 3; c = 1; d = 2

9. a = 1; b = 3; c = 2; d = 2

10. a = 2; b = 1; c = 1; d = 3

● What Your Score Means

10 to 16:

First-Impression Flaws!

While it's good to be your own person, it's also nice to put in the extra effort to be nice when you're meeting new people. As the saying goes, you only get one chance to make a first impression, so make it count. This does not mean you need to bend over backward to impress people. You can still be yourself—just add a friendly smile and let other people know that you're glad to meet them. First impressions do count, so give it a try!

17 to 23:

Nice Guys and Gals Do Finish First

You're right where you need to be—making great first impressions with all the people you meet. You're professional; you know when to put on a good show and when it's ok to relax. You realize that you've only got one chance to make the first impression, and you make sure it's a good one. When people say, "It was nice to meet you," they really mean it. Keep up the good work.

24 to 30:
First-Impression Overdrive

You always try to make a great first impression, but you may actually be trying a bit too hard. Be confident that people will like you for who you are. While it's always good to be friendly and courteous, there's no need to win over new people by buying gifts or going out of your way. It may in fact make people uncomfortable. Give people the chance to like you for you and the rest will follow.

What Is Your Body Language Saying to Potential Partners?

1. You typically wear outfits that:

    a. Are flattering and fit well

    b. Maximize your sex appeal

    c. Are frumpy and conservative

    d. Look funky to attract attention

2. When you notice someone staring at you from across the room, you:

    a. Look away embarrassed

    b. Stare right back and smile

    c. Lick your lips and approach

    d. Pretend you don't notice

3. Your posture when you walk is:

    a. Perfectly straight

    b. Slouched over

    c. Designed to highlight your assets

    d. Accented to give you a confident strut

4. When you are not interested in someone who approaches you, you generally:

    a. Say a quick hello and then turn away as quickly as possible

b. Talk for a little while anyway

c. Talk for a little while but keep a good distance between you and stand with your arms folded

d. Flirt away, because this person might have cute friends

5. When you are interested in someone who approaches you, you generally:

a. Slip your phone number into their pocket

b. Become embarrassed and stand closer to your friends

c. Lean forward to get as close as possible to the cutie

d. Flirt with other people to play hard to get

6. When you see someone who you are interested in that hasn't noticed you yet, you:

a. Try to get a friend to introduce you

b. March on over and say a friendly hello

c. Make eye contact and smile

d. Wait for the person to approach you

7. When a date puts a hand on your knee, you:

a. Brush it off

b. Respond favorably by holding the hand in yours

c. Seductively slide the hand farther up your leg

d. Pretend you don't notice

8. When you want a date to kiss you, you generally:

a. Wait patiently

b. Move in really close and give your hottest kiss-me look

c. Grab your date and plant one on the lips

d. Ask for the kiss

9. You consider yourself to be:

   a. Touchy-feely

   b. Someone who needs space

   c. Sexually charged

   d. Comfortable when close to others

10. When you sit, you typically:

   a. Cross your legs at the knee

   b. Let your legs fall wherever you find a comfortable position

   c. Cross your legs at the ankle

   d. Slide your leg over to play footsie with your date

Scoring:

1. a = 2; b = 3; c = 1; d = 2	**6.** a = 2; b = 3; c = 2; d = 1
2. a = 1; b = 2; c = 3; d = 1	**7.** a = 1; b = 2; c = 3; d = 1
3. a = 2; b = 1; c = 3; d = 3	**8.** a = 1; b = 2; c = 3; d = 2
4. a = 1; b = 2; c = 2; d = 3	**9.** a = 3; b = 1; c = 3; d = 2
5. a = 3; b = 1; c = 2; d = 3	**10.** a = 2; b = 1; c = 2; d = 3

● What Your Score Means

10 to 16:
Unapproachable and Unavailable

Your body language is saying, "Back off." That makes it difficult for someone to take the risk of trying to get to know you better. Perhaps you are coming across colder than you realize due to lack of confidence or fear of rejection. Consider smiling back across the room at someone instead of looking away or walking with a more confident, approachable posture. You may be scaring away potential partners before you've given them a chance.

17 to 23:
Worth Getting to Know

Your body language invites potential partners to take the risk of introducing themselves to you in the hopes of some further connection. You are able to succeed in the art of flirtation without making overt sexual advances that may give the wrong impression. Your confidence in yourself is indicated through your posture, eye-contact and charming smile and will attract attention from potential partners wherever you go.

24 to 30:
Take Me Home Tonight!

Your body language is saying that your hormones are pumping! With those bedroom eyes and skintight clothes, you are indicating to potential partners that you are available as well as comfortable with your sexuality. If this is the message you intend to portray, your body language is appropriate. However, if you are looking for more than a one-night stand, you may consider toning it down a notch to allow your potential partners to get to know the other, more complex sides to the person you are.

What Does Your Date's Body Language
Say to You?

1. On a date in a hot new restaurant, your date:

a. Gazes meaningfully into your eyes a couple of times during the evening

b. Stares at you all night long, barely looking down to eat

c. Hardly looks away from the plate

d. Checks out other attractive passersby but hardly notices you

2. While standing at a bar having drinks, your date:

a. Has hands all over you right away—even though you're not reciprocating

b. Avoids all physical contact

c. Occasionally touches you, like when someone needs to walk by

d. Gently puts an arm on your shoulder, which you hardly notice

3. You're at a party with people you hardly know when you get separated from your date. While across the room, your date:

a. Forgets you're there and spends a half hour chatting with friends

b. Looks up every few minutes to check that you are all right

   c. Immediately motions for you to come over if you're not intently talking to someone

   d. Smiles at you as you both talk to other people

4. You're at a party when you and your date decide to dance to a slow song. While dancing,

   a. There's enough room for another person or two to be dancing between you

   b. Your date draws you close and you sway cheek to cheek

   c. Your date holds you so tight that you can't breathe

   d. Your date looks at you for clues about how closely you want to dance

5. You're talking in a very soft voice about a private matter. Your date:

   a. Immediately says, "Speak up, I can't hear you!"

   b. Leans in a bit closer to hear you better

   c. Gently takes your arm and guides you to a less conspicuous place to protect your privacy

   d. Puts an arm around you and suggests leaving so you can speak more freely

6. When you go to the movies, your date:

   a. Sits beside you and doesn't move through the picture

   b. Leans over and whispers to you a few times

   c. Puts a hand on your knee

   d. Tries to kiss you in a romantic scene

7. You see a movie in which the couple happily comes together and gets married in the end. Your date:

   a. Walks stiffly and makes sure to leave space between you as you exit

   b. Slips a gentle arm around your waist as you walk out

   c. Holds your hand as you leave

   d. Tries to kiss you in your seat as the rest of the crowd shuffles out

8. The two of you are alone on the couch watching television.

   a. You look over and catch your date looking at you and s/he looks a little embarrassed

   b. Your date stays planted on one side of the sofa

   c. After a half hour, your date edges closer and rests a hand on your leg

   d. Your date has hands all over you from the minute you sit down and tries to kiss you before the first commercial

9. When you meet your date to go out, you notice the smell of:

   a. Overpowering cologne or perfume. It's almost breathtaking

   b. Alcohol. Smells like a brewery

   c. Nothing or subtle cologne

   d. Dirty socks and sweat

10. The two of you are about to go into a building. Your date:

   a. Runs ahead of you to open the door for you

   b. Opens the door, enters and lets the door slam in your face

c. Reaches forward and casually opens the door for you

d. Holds the door open for you after walking through

Scoring:

1. a = 2; b = 3; c = 1; d = 1	**6.** a = 1; b = 2; c = 2; d = 3
2. a = 3; b = 1; c = 2; d = 2	**7.** a = 1; b = 2; c = 2; d = 3
3. a = 1; b = 2; c = 3; d = 2	**8.** a = 2; b = 1; c = 2; d = 3
4. a = 1; b = 2; c = 3; d = 2	**9.** a = 3; b = 1; c = 2; d = 1
5. a = 1; b = 2; c = 2; d = 3	**10.** a = 3; b = 1; c = 2; d = 2

● What Your Score Means

10 to 16:
Body Language Is Lacking

Your date's body language does not say much. In general your date hasn't been very attentive to you and does not use his/her body to communicate. It's possible your date does have feelings for you but that physical expression does not come naturally. If this is the case you need to decide if this bothers you or if your date can change as you become closer to one another. Explore this issue if you continue to date . . . it may determine if this is the right person for you.

17 to 23:
Just Right Body Language

Your date's body language says "I like you" while respecting your need for your own physical space. This is a great balance because your date knows how to use physical expression without overwhelming you. Only time will tell if the relationship will work out. However, you have a good start to build upon. Your date seems to like being with you and treats you well . . . hopefully, there will be more good times to follow.

24 to 30:

Body Language Lust!

Your date likes you and is not afraid to show it! This person is ready to express these feelings physically in practically any time and place. While all this attention may be nice, it's really only enjoyable if there are feelings behind it . . . feelings that you both must feel. There's nothing wrong with feeling somewhat uncomfortable about all this physical expression. If your date does something you don't like, nip it in the bud before it goes too far. A few comments and the point will be clear. If not, think about dating someone else.

How Much Fun Are You on a Date?

1. What's your ideal first date?

    a. Brunch on the weekend

    b. Dinner at an intimate restaurant

    c. Meeting for a fast lunch or coffee during the week

    d. A few casual drinks after work

2. What do you wear on a first date?

    a. Something very conservative—you don't want to give your date the wrong idea

    b. Something in which you feel confident and comfortable

    c. Whatever is clean

    d. An outfit you purchased specially for the date

3. How would you best describe your date personality?

    a. Flirty

    b. Compassionate

    c. Contentious

    d. Outgoing

    e. Basically the same as my ordinary personality

4. Which of the following best describes your general attitude toward dating?

    a. It's a great way to spend my free time

b. The more dates I go on, the better chance I have of meeting someone I really like

c. It's a good way to get to know people

d. It's a necessary evil that you have to endure if you want to meet someone you like

5. Your meal was sub-par, but your date chose the restaurant. What do you say?

    a. You politely say that your meal was fine

    b. You comment on the great food

    c. You compliment the service and location

    d. You imply that it was not the best meal you've ever had

6. You know your date isn't going to be a love connection. What do you do?

    a. Grin and bear it: maybe your date has cute friends

    b. Make an excuse to leave and head home

    c. Flirt outrageously nonetheless, and never call your date again

    d. Call a bunch of friends and ask them to come join you

7. If conversation lags on a date, what do you usually do?

    a. Wait for your date to initiate a topic

    b. Launch into long tales of your accomplishments

    c. Ask questions about your date's interests

    d. Tell a funny story that you think is likely to start a new round of conversation

    e. Smile and move closer to your date and see what happens

8. What was the most frequent conversation topic on your last date?

   a. Recent movies that you've both seen

   b. Past loves and losses, with full sexual details

   c. The weather

   d. Your work and the places you've lived

   e. You can't even mention a topic—the conversation just went easily all night

9. If your date inquired about your dating history, you would:

   a. Tell provocative stories about your sexual exploits

   b. Reply that it was none of your date's business

   c. Get into the details of why your old relationships did not work out

   d. Offer a few polite details and move on

   e. Give as interesting an overview as possible and then ask a similar question

10. The evening of a great date is drawing to a close. What's on your mind?

   a. Gauging whether your date had as much fun as you did

   b. Coercing your date into bed

   c. Getting a good night's sleep

   d. How to make it clear that you want to see your date again

   e. How glad you are that you met a great person

11. How would your last date describe you?

   a. Quiet

   b. Fun

c. Reserved

d. Sensitive

e. A good listener

f. Entertaining

Scoring:

1. a = 2; b = 3; c = 1; d = 1

2. a = 1; b = 2; c = 1; d = 3

3. a = 3; b = 2; c = 1; d = 3; e = 2

4. a = 1; b = 2; c = 3; d = 1

5. a = 2; b = 3; c = 2; d = 1

6. a = 2; b = 1; c = 2; d = 3

7. a = 1; b = 1; c = 2; d = 3; e = 2

8. a = 2; b = 3; c = 1; d = 2; e = 3

9. a = 2; b = 1; c = 1; d = 2; e = 3

10. a = 2; b = 2; c = 1; d = 3; e = 3

11. a = 1; b = 3; c = 1; d = 2; e = 2; f = 2

● What Your Score Means

11 to 16:

You Are in Dating Dullsville

Your dates are not too exciting and often end early. Somehow, you find it difficult to make the leap from small talk to real conversation, and your dates rarely lead to real romance. It could be that negative experiences in past relationships have made you wary about romance. Or maybe it is simply your natural shyness or lack of self-esteem that lead you to become inhibited and withdrawn with new people. Either way, try to examine what the source of these feelings is. In the meantime, relax and think of a date as an opportunity for great conversation rather than a pressure situation. Dating can be fun and interesting, and a great way to meet new people.

17 to 22:

You Are Fun on a Date

You have a lot of energy and personality, and both of these are keys to great dates. You have the knack for making an evening memorable. Being flirtatious and outgoing are sure-fire ways to keep your date entertained. It is fabulous that you're able to see past the challenges of dating and enjoy it, but it's also important to remember that a great date involves a certain amount of give and take. You may want to let go of the need to be the center of attention, and make sure that you're listening to your date's signals. A good date is about connecting, rather than trying too hard to make an impression. On your next date, try toning it down a little and make a concentrated effort to listen to your date—you could be surprised at how well it goes.

23 to 28:

You Are a Great Date

You belong to a rare breed: people who have developed a knack for dating. You've found a great way to set the tone for a fun, relaxed evening. You understand that connecting and making conversation are critical elements to getting to know someone, but you aren't afraid to tell jokes and keep it light. Even if the person you're with doesn't seem like your dream partner, you consider it worthwhile to get to know them and to enjoy a pleasant, memorable evening together. Being a fun date is a great skill, and it probably means that your dates generally want to see you again. Lucky you!

29 to 33:

You Can Be Overpowering

You're sure to make a strong impression on your dates because you tend to come on with full force. While it's great that you feel comfortable with yourself and are willing to speak your mind, it's also important to recognize that there can be times when it's better to play it cool. It's possible that you may be coming on too strong in some cases and sending the wrong signals to your date. Additionally, by keeping your cool, you'll give yourself a better chance to get to know your companion and decide if this person is worth putting yourself into full gear.

Does Your Newest Love Interest Want You, Too?

1. After an evening together you usually hear from your new love interest:

  a. The morning of the following day

  b. The end of the following day

  c. A few days later

  d. You always make the call

  e. There's a message on your machine when you get home from the date

2. When you move in for a kiss, your crush answers by:

  a. Kissing back, sort of—you're not sure if it counts or not

  b. Offering a cheek

  c. Smooching like crazy

  d. Giving you a nice warm kiss

3. The person you're attracted to is:

  a. Single

  b. Married/formally committed

  c. Definitely looking for love

  d. Dating around

4. You flirt your heart out. Your new honey:

   a. Banters back

   b. Brings up an ex

   c. Talks about work

   d. Changes the subject

5. You mention an event that you'd like to go to together in a few weeks. Your new cutie:

   a. Mentions being extremely busy before you even say the date of the event

   b. Asks if you could make it a group thing

   c. Says no because work makes it impossible to plan too far ahead

   d. Smiles and accepts

   e. Mentions that he/she too would like to go to the same event, hinting that he/she'd like to join you

6. The two of you make eye contact:

   a. All the time

   b. Frequently

   c. Sometimes

   d. Rarely

   e. Never

7. When speaking to you, your potential honey:

   a. Sometimes touches you

b. Gets close to you without ever touching

c. Stands a couple of feet away

d. Apologizes if you accidentally brush hands

8. When you divulge something private about yourself, you get the sense that your love interest will remember it:

a. Definitely not

b. Probably not

c. Maybe

d. Probably

e. Definitely

9. While chatting with your crush you mention the bar that you and your friends plan to visit the following night. Your hottie:

a. Makes a brief appearance

b. Arrives before you do

c. Never shows

d. Stops by for a couple of drinks

10. When you tell a joke, the object of your desire:

a. Chuckles

b. Smiles

c. Laughs hard

d. Doesn't seem to get the funny

Scoring:

1. a = 1; b = 1; c = 2; d = 3; e = 3

2. a = 2; b = 3; c = 1; d = 1

3. a = 1; b = 3; c = 1; d = 2

4. a = 1; b = 2; c = 2; d = 3

5. a = 3; b = 3; c = 3; d = 1; e = 1

6. a = 1; b = 1; c = 2; d = 3; e = 3

7. a = 1; b = 2; c = 3; d = 2

8. a = 3; b = 3; c = 2; d = 1; e = 1

9. a = 2; b = 1; c = 3; d = 1

10. a = 2; b = 2; c = 1; d = 3

• What Your Score Means

10 to 16:

Love Is a Two-Way Street

It looks like looking for love has paid off—the one you want wants you back! There is abundant potential for getting closer and cozier; actions and reactions demonstrate not only a willingness to listen to you, but also an interest in paying you ardent attention. All signs indicate that your newest partner is ready to stay awhile. Revel in the reciprocity!

17 to 23:

Still a Maybe

One day you're sure that you both feel the fireworks, but the next day you're convinced that the chemistry is one-sided. Which feeling is right? Is this a yes or a no? Answering these questions is far from easy because you're getting mixed signals—ambiguity is the name of the game. If you can handle not knowing, then go along for the ride and see what happens. If you need to know where this will go, you'll have to open the lines of communication and discuss the way you feel. Just be sure before you ask any questions, that you're prepared to give and hear the answers!

24 to 30:

Seems Like a No-Go

Although you can never be sure unless you ask, it seems like this person does not share the special feelings that you're hoping for. It may be too early to tell but it seems that you two are not having an equal give-and-take. Your crush may like you very much but it seems like those feelings are more friendship than romance. Unless this person is playing an extreme game of hard to get, you're probably better off moving on. The sooner you end this relationship, the sooner you can meet someone who returns your desires and treats you the way you deserve to be treated.

What Are the Chances That Your Date Will Call You Back?

1. When you spoke to arrange the date, who suggested the date's activities?

    a. I did—my date seemed vague, and didn't have many ideas

    b. My date had planned out the entire evening, and told me that all I had to do was arrive

    c. We bounced around a few ideas, and then came to a consensus

    d. We both had strong ideas, and one of us begrudgingly gave in to the other

2. How would you best describe the overall mood on your date?

    a. Flirty

    b. Friendly and easy

    c. Argumentative

    d. Dull

    e. Congenial

3. How many times during the evening did one or the other of you burst out laughing?

    a. We seemed to be laughing the whole night

    b. I laughed politely once or twice

    c. Each of us laughed a few times

    d. Neither one of us really seemed to get that excited

4. What outward signs did you give your date that you were interested?

    a. I nodded and smiled a lot

    b. I asked a lot of questions and listened very closely

    c. None—I was basically pretty bored

    d. None—I was afraid to appear too eager

5. How would you describe the degree of sexual tension on your date?

    a. Steamy and intense

    b. There was some friction, but not huge sparks

    c. Warm and intimate

    d. Polite and cool

6. Which of the following is the closest to your date's final words?

    a. "I'll call you . . . sometime."

    b. "Are you free tomorrow night?"

    c. "This has been fun."

    d. "We should do this again."

    e. "It was really great to meet you."

    f. "It was nice to meet you."

7. Your date seems to want to tell revealing personal stories. How do you react?

    a. Nod and listen, trying to convey compassion

    b. Reply by telling stories of similar intimacy

c. Try to politely change the subject to lighter topics

d. Openly admit that the topic is too heavy and change the subject

8. During dinner, you glanced at your date while you thought you were both looking at your menus and deciding what to order. Your date was:

a. Looking into space

b. Glancing at the clock

c. Staring at you intensely

d. Smiling happily

9. How well do you feel that you held up your end of the conversation?

a. Not too well—occasionally I felt myself looking blankly at my date

b. I *was* the conversation

c. Well—I replied to my date's questions and vice versa

d. I didn't even notice—I was too busy having a good time!

10. Did your date seem comfortable making eye contact with you throughout the evening?

a. Certainly—in a casual, but friendly way

b. Absolutely—our eyes were locked most of the night

c. Not really—it was hard for us to catch one another's eye

d. Occasionally—although not always

Scoring:

1. a = 1; b = 3; c = 2; d = 1	**6.** a = 1; b = 3; c = 2; d = 2; e = 3; f = 1
2. a = 3; b = 3; c = 1; d = 1; e = 2	**7.** a = 3; b = 3; c = 2; d = 1
3. a = 3; b = 1; c = 2; d = 1	**8.** a = 2; b = 1; c = 3; d = 3
4. a = 2; b = 3; c = 1; d = 1	**9.** a = 1; b = 1; c = 2; d = 3
5. a = 3; b = 2; c = 3; d = 1	**10.** a = 2; b = 3; c = 1; d = 2

● What Your Score Means

10 to 16:
Doubtful Date

Don't be waiting for that phone to ring—and don't be surprised if it doesn't. It sounds as if your date was giving you the signs that the two of you didn't have a future. Think back over the evening and consider what you think are the reasons that the two of you didn't connect. If you just didn't have much in common, relax—you'll eventually meet the right person, and it'll be clear when you're both eager to go out again. Then again, if you think that some way that you acted might have set the date on the wrong course, examine why you do those things and try to avoid them on the next date. Even if this date was not a success you'll have many opportunities in the future to find the right person.

17 to 23:
Maybe Yes, Maybe No

It's not clear if this date will be coming back for more, simply because your time together sounds like it was ok—nothing more, nothing less. While your date wasn't a total disaster, it sounds as if you may have hit some rocky moments along the way. It still seems possible that your date might decide to give your connection another chance. If the two of you *do* go out again, concentrate on relaxing and being yourself. There's a comfortable space between appearing indifferent and appearing overeager, and it's in this space that romance starts to blossom.

24 to 30:
Coming Back for More!

Better warm up your sultry phone voice and get ready for your next date . . . it seems like a pretty sure thing that a date this great will bear repeating. Considering how well the two of you connected, it sounds as if your date will *definitely* call you back. Your date might not have been a perfect love connection, but it sounds like the two of you enjoyed each other's company and found plenty of common ground. If your date is interested in taking a chance, it seems likely that s/he will give you a call again . . . but remember you never really know what someone is thinking so give it a few days and if you don't get a call, it may be time to move on. Or, if you don't get a call, don't be afraid to initiate contact—call or email—some people expect the other side to make the first move. A simple, "Thanks, I had fun last night" might be in order. If you're afraid to make a call, you can leave a voicemail message when you know your date will not be home.

Are You Dating the Right Kind of People?

1. When it comes to politics, you and your latest date:

   a. Mostly concur but occasionally debate ideas

   b. Don't agree on anything

   c. Agree on everything

   d. Disagree often but have great discussions

2. If you made a list of the top ten attributes you wanted in a partner, your most recent date would have:

   a. None of them

   b. All of them

   c. Some of them

   d. Most of them

3. When listening to the radio, you and your dates typically:

   a. Battle over which station to choose

   b. Take turns picking the music

   c. Always agree on the tunes

   d. End up turning it off because agreeing on one station is too stressful

4. Your date thought your favorite book:

   a. Was the most brilliant thing ever written

b. Sounded intriguing

c. Was awful

d. Was interesting

f. Sounded boring

5. When meeting your current honey for your annual office party, you figure that s/he will be:

a. Wearing a just-right outfit

b. Dressed inappropriately

c. Looking so gorgeous you might not make it through the party

d. You have no idea what to expect

6. The last time you introduced a date to your parents, they were:

a. Pleased

b. Disappointed

c. Thrilled

d. Neutral

7. Your friends like the people you date:

a. Always

b. Often

c. Sometimes

d. Rarely

e. Never

8. After your last date, you:

a. Smiled for days

b. Felt really insecure until your date called a few days later

c. Did not think about the evening

d. Phoned your friends to help interpret how it went

9. When you kiss someone for the first time, you usually feel:

a. Fine

b. Happy

c. Very excited

d. Curious

10. When picking a movie to rent, you and your date usually:

a. Compromise

b. Take turns choosing

c. Go straight for the same section of the video store

d. Fight

Scoring:

1. a = 2; b = 3; c = 1; d = 1	**6.** a = 1; b = 3; c = 1; d = 2
2. a = 3; b = 1; c = 2; d = 2	**7.** a = 1; b = 1; c = 2; d = 3; e = 3
3. a = 3; b = 2; c = 1; d = 3	**8.** a = 1; b = 3; c = 3; d = 2
4. a = 1; b = 2; c = 3; d = 2; e = 3	**9.** a = 3; b = 1; c = 1; d = 2
5. a = 2; b = 3; c = 1; d = 2	**10.** a = 2; b = 2; c = 1; d = 3

● What Your Score Means

10 to 16:
Attracting the Right Type

When it comes to partner picking, you gravitate toward people who are right for you. You and your dates often have similar backgrounds, tastes and interests that make hanging out not only fun, but also relatively trouble-free. No need to fight over which restaurant to visit—you're already of the same opinion; and if not you two compromise effortlessly. No need to stress over whose turn it is to pay—you've easily established a system that works for both of you. Congratulations on determining what matters to you in a partner and then seeking it out—you choose people with whom you get along beautifully. Now it's just a matter of finding that one who shines even brighter than the rest. . . .

17 to 23:
Hit or Miss

You date a wide variety of people and don't have a solid pattern finding or overlooking the ones who are best for you. It's great that you're open-minded and willing to give people a chance even if they don't fit an ideal picture of the person you're looking to meet. While this is a great attitude, it may help you find romance if you start to think about the qualities that make you happy and why. You must remember that finding the right person is a process, and not necessarily an easy one. Sometimes you've got to go through some bad relationships in order to realize what's so great about the good ones. With each new relationship, whether it's full of fun or terribly tedious, you're learning about what you want, what you like and what you need. Keep dating and soon you'll figure out what you want and then you'll be able to find it.

24 to 30:

Not Attracting the Right Ones

Sometimes it's hard to put a finger on what brings two people together. In your case, it's pretty difficult to figure out why you date the people you do. Frequently, it seems that you and your dates are at odds with each other. Differences of opinion don't necessarily foreshadow doom in your relationships, of course; in addition to being stimulating, conflict can challenge and teach you in ways that peace and ease cannot. The key is to be aware that you have choices: You can continue to date people with whom you clash, or you can forego the strife and stress and date people more in tune with you. Excitement or serenity? It's up to you to decide which one matters most.

Your Romantic Personality

Wouldn't the mating game be much easier if you could recognize where you blossom and where you may tend to wilt? Navigating the world of love and romance is much easier when you have a strong understanding of your romantic personality.

Once you have a better understanding of your romantic self, you can examine what's behind your behavior and gain a clearer sense of how you affect the people around you. Are you making an impression on the people you meet at work, at parties and at the grocery store? And if so, exactly what kind of impression are you leaving behind? Spend some time on the surveys in this section and you'll see what you're doing now and what changes you can make that will help you meet Mr. or Ms. Right.

How Romantic Are You?

1. Your six-month anniversary with your significant other is coming up in one week. As a gift, you will:

    a. Do nothing. You're not into the whole gift thing

    b. Run out that day to get a card—you always leave things like that to the last minute

    c. Shop around for the next few days to find a gift you know your partner will love

    d. Relax. You've already bought a gift and planned a special celebration for the occasion

2. Your pet name for your significant other is:

    a. Any cute name that you can imagine

    b. Honey

    c. His/her given name

    d. Baby

3. It's Friday night, and you've got a date with your partner. What are your ideal plans?

    a. Watching a romantic video while cuddling by the light of scented candles

    b. Getting together with your partner and a bunch of good friends

    c. Getting dressed up for a night that will include good wine, a fine meal, dancing and a moonlit stroll

   d. Staying in with a warm bath drawn for two, followed by a sensual full-body massage, topped with champagne and strawberries

4. Massage is best:

   a. When my partner does it for me every day after work

   b. When my partner and I do it for each other whenever we're stressed

   c. When done with love, tenderness and a little massage oil

   d. When done with massage oil by candlelight with soft music playing in the background

5. Your partner wants to cuddle. You:

   a. Oblige and cuddle your honey

   b. Try to avoid it whenever possible—you're not a cuddly type of person

   c. Snuggle right up. You'd be in heaven if you could just cuddle all day

   d. Cuddle even though you don't enjoy it; it's one of the surest ways to get to sex

6. You and your partner have had a bad fight. You know you were clearly in the wrong, and you admit it. Your partner was very hurt and upset. How would you apologize?

   a. With a simple, "I know I was wrong and I'm sorry. Can we get over this?"

   b. By singing "I'm sorry" on your partner's answering machine every few hours and sending a plant to express your regret

   c. By bringing flowers and saying something like, "I'm sorry. Please let's not fight like this ever again."

d. By having a long talk about how you were wrong, and that you're sorry, and then making up with a lot of affection

7. For your honey's birthday, you decide to pick up:

a. Something practical that can be used often

b. Something that my partner really wants and will enjoy while thinking of me

c. A new watch, dinner at the finest restaurant in town, a dozen roses, more than anything he or she would possibly ask for, because your partner deserves the best

d. Something that has sentimental value for both of you—along with a thoughtful card, which may also be accompanied by some flowers

8. When it comes to celebrating anniversaries, you like to:

a. Celebrate the anniversary of the day you met, every month for the first year and then once a year

b. Celebrate the anniversary of the day you became a couple, the day you first kissed, the day you first met, the first time you said "I love you," etc.

c. Hope your partner hints about it the week before, because you can never remember anniversaries

d. Celebrate the anniversary of the day you became a couple every year

9. When you think about Valentine's Day, you consider it:

a. A greeting-card holiday, used only as a way to make money for companies selling cards, candy and flowers

b. A perfect excuse to celebrate your love

c. A day when you're expected to do things for each other

d. It's the most romantic and fun day of the year!

10. You say "I love you" to your partner:

a. Every day

b. As much as possible

c. You're not ready to say it yet, but once you get there it will be nice to say!

d. Never

11. And when you say "I love you":

a. You really mean it

b. You like to be poetic and add little things like, "with all my heart" or "forever and ever"

c. You're only saying it back so your partner doesn't feel uncomfortable having said it first

d. You're only saying it to get your partner into bed

Scoring:

1. a = 1; b = 1; c = 2; d = 3

2. a = 3; b = 2; c = 1; d = 2

3. a = 2; b = 1; c = 3; d = 3

4. a = 1; b = 2; c = 2; d = 3

5. a = 2; b = 1; c = 3; d = 1

6. a = 1; b = 3; c = 2; d = 2

7. a = 1; b = 2; c = 3; d = 2

8. a = 2; b = 3; c = 1; d = 2

9. a = 1; b = 2; c = 1; d = 3

10. a = 2; b = 3; c = 2; d = 1

11. a = 2; b = 3; c = 1; d = 1

• What Your Score Means

11 to 17:
Out of Touch Much?

If romance were a snake, you wouldn't have to worry about getting bitten, because you're nowhere near it. Unless your partner has expressly told you that your relationship does not need romance, you may want to show your honey that you have a sensitive side. Even small gestures every once in a while can have a big impact. Surprise your sweetie with flowers, a thoughtful card or by making an effort to cuddle. When you take the initiative to show you care, your partner will appreciate it and may even do the same. Instead of buying a practical gift for your significant other's birthday, try to be creative and find something with sentimental value. The key is to express your feelings in a way that feels comfortable and be sure that your efforts are sincere.

18 to 25:
Romantic Romeo / Gentle Juliet

Congratulations! You have mastered the art of being romantic without going completely overboard. Your friends probably tell you that you two make a cute couple because you can show that you care for one another without making other people feel uncomfortable. You've learned that little things like spelling out "I love you" in M&Ms can be just as romantic—if not more so—than a candlelit dinner at an exclusive restaurant. Although you're doing well now, be careful not to get lazy. Try to keep things creative and spontaneous. Don't limit your romantic gestures to holidays and anniversaries—let each other know how you feel each and every day. Try to do something special for each other once a week, and remember that romance does not need to be something that one person does for the other. You can both plan a romantic activity and then enjoy it together.

26 to 33:
A Hopeless Romantic and Then Some!

You like everything in your relationship to be champagne and rose petals, and while it's good to believe in the fairytale, be sure that you're not basing your whole relationship on grand gestures. You should be able to spend time together with your feet on the ground instead of your head in the clouds. While romance can be hypnotic, every now and then you need to touch base with reality and make sure you're in love with a real person and not just in love with the romance. With that caution in mind, enjoy the fact that you have found someone who gives you romantic inspiration. In today's fast-paced, hectic world, it is a rare treat to find someone who takes the time and effort to be such a thoughtful partner. Keep up the good work and remember to make sure that there are genuine feelings behind all the romantic things that you do.

How Sexually Aggressive Are You?

1. You're at a party where you don't know many people, so you decide to approach someone to start a conversation. Who do you pick?

   a. The best-dressed

   b. The loneliest

   c. The funniest

   d. The best-looking

2. You're out with friends and run into a good-looking person who you've never really liked. It's a slow night and you wind up talking anyway. At the end of the night, you:

   a. Agree to go out with this person, just in case s/he's not as annoying as you think

   b. Ask this person to go home with you, because, hey, a great body is a great body

   c. Walk away wondering why you just wasted the last hour

   d. Give in to a good-night kiss—you don't need to be in love to enjoy a little smooching!

3. At the end of a great first date, you put your hand on your date's shoulder and lean forward looking for a kiss good night. If your date does not respond, you:

   a. Forget the kiss and say good-bye

   b. Try to plant a kiss anyway and hope your date reciprocates

c. Lean in a little closer and see if you get a response

d. Ask for the kiss

4. If you polled your friends to find out your reputation, they would say:

a. That you can hold your own in the dating world and are no pushover

b. That you are considered sweet and innocent, and would make a great spouse

c. That you make Madonna look like a nun

d. That you'd be happier if you knew the last name of every person you've been with

5. Which of the following is closest to your idea of a great night out?

a. Bringing a cute date back to your place for some late-night hanky-panky

b. Trying a new sexual position

c. Having a leisurely meal with your close friends at your favorite restaurant

d. Meeting someone you may want to date

6. When you are in bed with someone, do you:

a. Initiate the action by removing your lover's clothes

b. Allow your partner to dictate the pace

c. Slap a hand away if things get too frisky

d. Try not to think too much and just let things happen

7. Which of the following most closely resembles the sexiest thing you would do to get someone's attention?

   a. Move your clothing in a suggestive way to show off your tan lines

   b. Wink and blow a kiss

   c. Blush

   d. Smile across a room at someone you've never met

8. What signal do you want your clothes and general appearance to send to potential love interests?

   a. "Come and get me, baby."

   b. "What do you want to name our children?"

   c. "I look good, don't I?"

   d. "I'm friendly and confident."

9. Picture all the people you've ever slept with being in one place. If you could fit them all into one vehicle, what would it be?

   a. A motorcycle

   b. A Volkswagen bug

   c. A minivan

   d. A tour bus

   e. A 747

10. What is the first thing you think when you wake up in bed with someone for the first time?

   a. "What's his/her name?"

b. "I can't wait to spend my life with this person."

c. "I'm so excited that we finally spent the night together!"

d. "I'm so glad that we could spend the night just cuddling."

Scoring:

1. a = 2; b = 1; c = 2; d = 3	**6.** a = 3; b = 2; c = 1; d = 2
2. a = 2; b = 3; c = 1; d = 2	**7.** a = 3; b = 2; c = 1; d = 1
3. a = 1; b = 3; c = 2; d = 2	**8.** a = 3; b = 1; c = 2; d = 2
4. a = 2; b = 1; c = 3; d = 3	**9.** a = 1; b = 2; c = 2; d = 3; e = 3
5. a = 3; b = 3; c = 1; d = 2	**10.** a = 3; b = 1; c = 2; d = 1

● What Your Score Means

10 to 16:
You Are Reserved in the Bedroom

You tend to be careful in the bedroom rather than aggressive and experimental. Being completely comfortable with yourself and your partner makes sex much more satisfying, both physically and emotionally, so do what works for you. But realize that while you can't be too careful, you may miss out on exciting times by locking yourself in your room. Try to live life to the fullest without compromising your standards and morals.

17 to 23:
You Are a Flirty and Fun Lover

You are confident enough to party hard and get close to people, but also know when to draw the line and pull back. Believe it or not, people respect that. Get to know them first and let them get to know you, and then you have a chance to build a strong relationship (if that's what you want). Sometimes you have to take chances in life in order to get the rewards, and you seem willing and able to do that. As long as you carefully assess the risks, why not go for some excitement once in a while?

24 to 30:

You Are an Adventuresome Lover

While you may be enjoying your life as it is, it might be a good idea to consider channeling some of your energy into some productive endeavors OUTSIDE the bedroom. Being outgoing and aggressive are traits that can be used to your benefit in lots of areas, including at work or in building friendships. No need to change your personality, but you may want to alter some of your bedroom habits. You want to be sure that people are interested in you for your personality and character, not your propensity to jump into bed. On the other hand, if you are focusing your sexual assertiveness on one person and you are responsible, then keep at it and enjoy.

Are You a Flirt?

1. When you go out with friends, do you:

   a. Dress up, but keep it conservative

   b. Wear sexy clothes

   c. Dress comfortably and casually

   d. Wear anything that will draw attention

2. When you see someone attractive, do you:

   a. Go up and comment on their good looks

   b. Stare from across the room, hoping your eyes will meet

   c. Slip this hottie your phone number as you pass by

   d. Make casual conversation to try to find out if this one's single

   e. Do nothing but hope that s/he approaches you

3. You're at a party and you're not particularly interested in your date. Do you:

   a. Become a social butterfly and talk to everyone, especially single people

   b. Give your date your full attention

   c. Scan the room for attractive people and make sure to introduce yourself to them before you leave

   d. Make eye contact with attractive people, but don't initiate conversation

4. Not including the clothes you have to wear for work, is most of your wardrobe:

- **a.** Casual and conservative
- **b.** Somewhat revealing and/or tight
- **c.** Cool and fashionable
- **d.** Very sexy

5. If you were attracted to someone who was already involved in a relationship, would you:

- **a.** Do nothing
- **b.** Dress in a way that is sure to call attention
- **c.** Make "suggestive" comments whenever you can
- **d.** Try to be around this person as much as possible, hoping that s/he'll notice you and make a move
- **e.** Make it clear that you're interested

6. How many times have your friends commented about your flirtatious ways?

- **a.** Never
- **b.** Once or twice
- **c.** A few times
- **d.** Too many times to count

7. How often do you find yourself flirting with someone?

- **a.** Never
- **b.** Rarely

c. Sometimes

d. Frequently

8. If you were involved in a relationship and someone really attractive flirted with you, would you:

a. Flirt back—it's all just innocent fun, right?

b. Ignore it

c. Let them know you are in a relationship

d. Give them your phone number

9. You normally flirt with:

a. Anyone who flirts with you

b. Anyone attractive

c. Only people who make you feel comfortable

d. Only people who you would like to date

10. If you were at a bar and you spotted someone really attractive, would you:

a. Buy them a drink

b. Accidentally bump into them, smile and start a conversation

c. Go up to them and use your best pickup line

d. Do nothing

11. Do you flirt:

a. For the fun of it

b. To get someone to ask you out

c. To show someone you're interested

d. To see how many people you can attract

Scoring:

1. a = 1; b = 3; c = 1; d = 2	7. a = 1; b = 1; c = 2; d = 3
2. a = 3; b = 1; c = 3; d = 2; e = 1	8. a = 2; b = 1; c = 1; d = 3
3. a = 3; b = 1; c = 3; d = 2	9. a = 3; b = 3; c = 2; d = 1
4. a = 1; b = 2; c = 2; d = 3	10. a = 2; b = 2; c = 3; d = 1
5. a = 1; b = 2; c = 3; d = 2; e = 3	11. a = 2; b = 2; c = 1; d = 3
6. a = 1; b = 2; c = 2; d = 3	

• What Your Score Means

11 to 17:

You Are a Reserved Rookie

You tend to be somewhat reserved when it comes to flirting. You are fairly shy in nature, and you usually don't approach people you find attractive because you are afraid of the possibility of rejection. You prefer to wait for others to approach you first, because it helps you to relax and come out of your shell. When you do flirt, you do so because you are interested in someone and it is often someone who you have met before. You take a conservative and subtle approach to flirting, such as smiling a lot or making casual conversation. Unfortunately, your potential mates may not get the hint that you are interested. You may need to be a little more direct in order to get what you want.

18 to 25:

You Are a Fun Flirt

You love to flirt because it's fun, and it's an easy way to break the ice with new people. You tend to be subtle in your approach—

when you find someone attractive, you do what you can to get their attention without being too blunt or forward. You usually limit your flirting to those people whom you are really interested in getting to know better. When you go out, you like to look good and try to draw the attention of potential dates. Just remember that there is more to people than first meets the eye, and you could be walking right past a great person in your attempt to meet that hottie across the room.

26 to 33:
You Are a Super Seducer

Some people might call you a player or a tease. You flirt with anyone you find attractive, often just to see what response you can get. You are forward and direct in your approach to the opposite sex, and you don't waste a lot of time with subtleties. You like to be the center of attention, and you tend to dress in a manner that is sure to get you noticed. Your seductive style gets you a lot of dates, but you also leave a lot of broken hearts behind. You may want to slow down a little and save your flirting for the really special ones. You may be risking earning the reputation of being nothing more than frivolous and losing the opportunity to get into the right kind of serious relationship.

How Promiscuous Are You?

1. I know the last name of every person I've ever slept with.

    a. True—and the middle name, too!

    b. True

    c. Almost true

    d. False

    e. False—I don't even know the first name of every person I've slept with!

2. People call me after we fool around.

    a. Always

    b. Usually

    c. Sometimes

    d. Rarely

    e. Never

3. I kiss on the first date.

    a. Always

    b. Usually

    c. Sometimes

    d. Rarely

    e. Never

4. I always have a supply of condoms—even when I'm single.

    a. True

    b. False

5. My parents couldn't name any of my last partners.

    a. True

    b. False

6. My friends have described my lovers as "patient."

    a. True

    b. False

7. It's no big deal to fool around with a friend's ex.

    a. True

    b. False

8. I always wear good underwear on blind dates—you never know.

    a. True

    b. False

9. I've often been called a "tease."

    a. True

    b. False

10. After a night out, I've gone to work wearing yesterday's clothes.

    a. True

    b. False

11. I've called out the wrong name in a moment of passion.

    a. True

    b. False

Scoring:

1. a = 1; b = 1; c = 2; d = 3; e = 3	7. a = 2; b = 1
2. a = 1; b = 1; c = 2; d = 3; e = 3	8. a = 2; b = 1
3. a = 3; b = 3; c = 2; d = 1; e = 1	9. a = 2; b = 1
4. a = 2; b = 1	10. a = 2; b = 1
5. a = 2; b = 1	11. a = 2; b = 1
6. a = 1; b = 2	

● What Your Score Means

11 to 14:

You Are Pretty Prudish

You're very selective about getting physical. Partners describe you as "nice," and they often invite you to family functions. Are you uncomfortable with your sexuality, scared of intimacy or just waiting for the right person? Getting physically close can be a very special experience—as long as it's the right person at a pace that makes you feel comfortable. No need to speed it up. Just make sure that you are keeping it slow for the right reasons.

15 to 19:

You Are a Discriminating Dater

You know you have a passionate side, but you aren't comfortable showing it to just anyone. Your past is nothing to be ashamed of, but it's not boring either. Congratulations—you've managed to achieve a great balance between healthy learning experiences and good old-fashioned values. Keep having fun—selectively!

20 to 25:
You Are Pretty Promiscuous

Slow down for a minute and think about why you're leading this promiscuous lifestyle. Do you feel like sex is all you have to offer? It's okay to be adventuresome and have some fun, but maybe you're not giving yourself enough credit. Sex is not the only way to get close to someone—you have a lot more to offer.

Is Love at First Sight a Possibility for You?

1. You are invited to a party where you will not know many of the people. You will most likely:

    a. Spend the evening having brief chats with a few of the other guests

    b. Not attend

    c. Go to the party, but probably leave after half an hour

    d. Stand a good chance of making new friends

2. How important is fashion to you?

    a. Extremely

    b. Very

    c. Somewhat

    d. Not at all

3. Which word would your friends say best describes you?

    a. Caring

    b. Funny

    c. Outgoing

    d. Reserved

4. Physical attraction is:

    a. An important part of any relationship

b. The reason people are drawn to each other

c. Something that can increase the more people know each other

d. Something that diminishes the longer a relationship lasts

5. After meeting a great person at a party who seemed like your ideal mate, you tell your friends:

a. I'm in love

b. I met someone really special and I really want to make it work

c. I met someone great but will take things slowly

d. Nothing—why mention it when you only hung out one night?

6. After meeting a new person, you tend to remember:

a. What you told the person about yourself

b. What most interested you about the other person

c. What you have in common

d. What about the conversation most engaged the other person

7. How opinionated are you?

a. Extremely

b. Somewhat

c. It depends on the subject

d. Not at all

8. You compare the people you meet against your concept of an "ideal type":

a. Always

b. Often

   c. Sometimes

   d. Rarely

   e. Never

9. When you look at people the first thing you notice is:

   a. Their clothes

   b. Their body type

   c. Their face

   d. Their reaction to you

10. Which animal best describes your personality:

   a. A kitty cat

   b. A puppy dog

   c. A peacock

   d. A shark

Scoring:

1. a = 2; b = 1; c = 2; d = 3	**6.** a = 1; b = 3; c = 2; d = 3
2. a = 1; b = 2; c = 3; d = 3	**7.** a = 1; b = 2; c = 2; d = 3
3. a = 3; b = 2; c = 3; d = 1	**8.** a = 1; b = 2; c = 3; d = 4; e = 5
4. a = 3; b = 3; c = 2; d = 1	**9.** a = 1; b = 2; c = 3; d = 3
5. a = 3; b = 3; c = 2; d = 1	**10.** a = 2; b = 3; c = 1; d = 1

• What Your Score Means

10 to 16:
Love at First Sight Seems Unlikely

We all enter into love and relationships in different ways, and "love at first sight" may not be the form that most fits your personality. Some people take longer to get to know others and open up to them and, in turn, let other people open up as well. The reason why this may be the case is not necessarily the point, as it is by no means an issue of "good" or "bad." It is just a matter of knowing your own style and creating situations that will put you in the best position to achieve your goals. If you are looking for love, try not to rush the process. If you sense a seed of interest in another person, allow time for growth. You appear to be a person who prefers to build strong relationships one step at a time, and if you focus too much on finding that spark right from the start you may miss what is waiting for you around the corner.

17 to 23:
Love at First Sight Could Happen to You

It appears that you are no stranger to the excitement that can come with a sense of immediate connection to another person. You have the capacity to be open to new people, while also allowing others in the room to get to know you as well. But, ask yourself this one question: "Do I sometimes second-guess myself after the initial intensity of that first meeting?" Love at first sight isn't just about the moment of convergence, but the trust in that moment that sustains the process that follows. Keep an eye on whether or not you hit a dip in the road somewhere after that moment of discovery. Only time, and experience, will tell if your "love at first sight" will go the distance.

24 to 32:

Love at First Sight Is for You!

In the immortal words of Sam Cooke, "Cupid, draw back your bow." If you haven't experienced love at first sight, chances are good that you will at some point. You are not only able to connect with others, but you approach new people with an open mind. This quality makes the chances of finding love fast very strong. If you don't have your mind already made up about who you are looking for, you stand a much better chance of seeing each new person for what he or she has to offer. And that's the magic equation: a personality that seeks out people and a nonjudgmental openness when you meet them. So, keep your eyes and ears and heart open—and trust the moment when the time comes.

How's Your Sex Life?

1. How often do you discuss your sex life with your partner?

   a. Often

   b. Occasionally

   c. Rarely

   d. Never

2. In terms of experiencing "pleasure" (i.e., reaching climax), you think it's most important that:

   a. Your partner is pleased

   b. You're pleased

   c. Both of you are equally pleased

   d. Both of you enjoy yourselves, but reaching orgasm is not crucial

3. When you have a steady sexual partner, how often do have sexual encounters?

   a. Several times a day, if possible

   b. Several times a week, if possible

   c. A few times a month

   d. Once a month, at most

4. When it comes to sexual creativity, you and your partner:

   a. Are too embarrassed to try anything new

b. Experiment occasionally

c. Experiment as much as possible

d. Do not feel that a "creative effort" is necessary . . . sex should just naturally occur

5. How do you feel about telling your lover what you enjoy sexually?

a. You are too embarrassed to do so

b. You give subtle hints

c. You are eager to tell your partner what pleases you

d. You tell only if your partner asks

6. Your favorite sexual mood is:

a. Wild, crazy and exciting

b. Romantic and sweet

c. Quick and easy

d. A mixture of the above, depending on your mood at the time

7. Your thoughts about foreplay are:

a. It's a waste of time

b. It's a fun way to get both of you in the mood

c. A little foreplay never hurts

d. It depends on your mood

8. If you're "in the mood" but your partner isn't, you:

a. Are upset and disappointed

b. Are understanding and happy to snuggle instead

c. Do what it takes to get your partner in the mood

d. Don't care much

9. How much of a sexual tease are you?

   a. You are a master at it

   b. You tease a little for the fun of it

   c. It depends on whether or not your partner likes to be teased

   d. You are not at all a sexual tease

10. If you want to spice up your sex life, you're most likely to try:

   a. Wearing sexy clothing

   b. Doing a strip tease

   c. Using sexual toys

   d. Watching pornography

   e. Trying a new position

   f. Nothing special—that's not your style

11. Your feelings about sexual toys are:

   a. They're disgusting!

   b. You have a whole collection!

   c. Some are fun, but some are a little TOO much for your taste

   d. You have a few body oils and other "mild" toys

   e. They're just not for you

Scoring:

1. a = 3; b = 2; c = 1; d = 1	7. a = 1; b = 3; c = 2; d = 2
2. a = 1; b = 1; c = 3; d = 3	8. a = 3; b = 2; c = 3; d = 1
3. a = 3; b = 2; c = 1; d = 1	9. a = 3; b = 2; c = 2; d = 1
4. a = 1; b = 2; c = 3; d = 2	10. a = 2; b = 3; c = 3; d = 3; e = 2; f = 1
5. a = 1; b = 2; c = 3; d = 2	
6. a = 3; b = 2; c = 1; d = 2	11. a = 1; b = 3; c = 2; d = 3; e = 2

● **What Your Score Means**

11 to 18:
Your Sex Life Is Lacking

You are not enjoying your sex life as much as you could. If you do have sex, you treat it more like a "chore" than something fun and fulfilling. Have you explored why you feel this way about sex? Perhaps you haven't found a partner who makes you feel comfortable enough to truly enjoy yourself. Sex can be a wonderful experience if you share it with the right person. Don't give up on it just yet. Do some investigation to see why you feel the way you do and talk to your partner about ways to make you more comfortable. Give it a try—your sex life may thank you for it!

19 to 26:
You Are a Romantic Lover

You are a romantic when it comes to your sex life. You like the mood to be just right so that your sexual activities are sweet, romantic and loving. Yet, you are able to dabble in the wild and exciting sexual arena when you need something a little different and creative. You're comfortable and satisfied with your sex life, and you know you have the proper attitude to be a great lover.

27 to 33:
You Are a Sexual Adventurer

When it comes to sex, you're willing to try anything and everything, and as a result you have a creative and fulfilling sex life. You clearly enjoy sex and have the confidence to be an assertive and fun sexual partner. However, it's also important to remember that while sex is fun, it can also be a meaningful and loving experience. It will enhance your sex life and your relationships if you can also enjoy the emotional component of sexual relations. Investigate this aspect of sex . . . you may be surprised by what you find.

Are You over Your Ex?

1. You look through pictures of the two of you but promise yourself it's the last time.

   a. Always

   b. Often

   c. Sometimes

   d. Rarely

   e. Never

2. When you get good or bad news, your ex is the first person you want to call.

   a. Always

   b. Often

   c. Sometimes

   d. Rarely

   e. Never

3. You've broken off a relationship with someone new without a good reason.

   a. Always

   b. Often

   c. Sometimes

   d. Rarely

   e. Never

4. Even though you want to be intimate with someone else, you can't imagine actually doing it.

   a. Always

   b. Often

   c. Sometimes

   d. Rarely

   e. Never

5. You "casually" bring up your ex in conversations with your friends.

   a. Always

   b. Often

   c. Sometimes

   d. Rarely

   e. Never

6. There are several places you avoid because of the attached memories to them.

   a. Always

   b. Often

   c. Sometimes

   d. Rarely

   e. Never

7. You have dreams that you are still together.

   a. Always

   b. Often

c. Sometimes

d. Rarely

e. Never

8. When you come home late after a night out drinking, you are tempted to call your ex.

a. Always

b. Often

c. Sometimes

d. Rarely

e. Never

9. You've cried about your breakup on Valentine's Day, New Year's Eve, your anniversary, your partner's birthday or other holidays.

a. Always

b. Often

c. Sometimes

d. Rarely

e. Never

10. Would you decline a friend's wedding invitation because you don't want to go alone?

a. Definitely

b. Maybe

c. Probably not

d. Definitely not

11. You write letters to your ex because there are still thoughts and feelings you want to express.

    a. Often

    b. Sometimes

    c. Rarely

    d. Never

Scoring:

1. a = 3; b = 3; c = 2; d = 1; e = 1

2. a = 3; b = 3; c = 2; d = 1; e = 1

3. a = 3; b = 3; c = 2; d = 1; e = 1

4. a = 3; b = 3; c = 2; d = 1; e = 1

5. a = 3; b = 3; c = 2; d = 1; e = 1

6. a = 3; b = 3; c = 2; d = 1; e = 1

7. a = 3; b = 3; c = 2; d = 1; e = 1

8. a = 3; b = 3; c = 2; d = 1; e = 1

9. a = 3; b = 3; c = 2; d = 1; e = 1

10. a = 3; b = 2; c = 2; d = 1

11. a = 3; b = 2; c = 2; d = 1

• What Your Score Means

11 to 18:

You Are Braveheart

Congratulations! Recovering from a breakup with a loved one is one of the most difficult processes a person can go through, but you are well on your way to emotional health. You are ready to move on and find your next sweetheart. You don't need much advice, although if you know anyone struggling with this issue, you may want to give them a call and let them cry on your shoulder.

19 to 26:

You Are on an Emotional Roller Coaster

This is a tough stage because there are times when you think you have moved on, but then something triggers a relapse. A sure sign of not being over your ex is when you say, "I am totally over him/her." You need to clarify your goals: Do you want to enter another relationship, or are you more interested in just hanging out and having fun? A break between relationships can be healthy, but we can't control the timing of fate. The bottom line is to trust your instincts—they're right more often than you may think.

27 to 33:

You Are the Kleenex Kid

The bad part of what you're going through is that there really isn't anything that can make you feel better in the short run (other than perhaps a reconciliation). But the good news is that the cliché is true: Time really does heal all wounds. And that healing process can be sped up if you keep yourself busy. Take on activities that you enjoy and that bolster your self-esteem. Start working out, take up painting, try to learn a foreign language, or take that trip to Europe you've always wanted. Your friends will want you to start dating right away; if you feel up to it that's fine, but there's no reason to rush. You'll know when you're ready.

Can You Be Friends with Your Ex?

1. The mere thought of seeing your ex again makes you feel:

   a. Nauseous

   b. Nervous

   c. Excited

   d. Angry

2. Your friend reports that your ex has been observed cuddling up with a new love interest. You feel:

   a. Genuinely happy for your ex

   b. Slightly hurt and betrayed

   c. Vengeful

   d. Bummed for a little while

3. When you bump into your ex in the supermarket, you:

   a. Avoid eye contact and pass by as if nothing happened

   b. Leave immediately

   c. Manage to carry on a semblance of a normal conversation with your ex

   d. Feel a little awkward, but smile and say hello

4. How long has it been since you and your ex broke up?

   a. One day—one month

b. One month–six months

c. Six months–one year

d. Over a year

5. Why did you break up?

    a. You and your ex both realized that your relationship wasn't working out

    b. You and your ex had a huge fight and said things that couldn't be taken back

    c. You (or your ex) cheated

    d. You mutually agreed to end your relationship to save your friendship with each other

    e. One of you was unhappy

6. By what means was your relationship with your ex dissolved?

    a. Over the phone

    b. By email

    c. With a face-to-face conversation

    d. By court order

7. If you had the opportunity to get back together with your ex, you would:

    a. Work on establishing a friendship instead

    b. Jump at the chance

    c. Not even consider it for a nanosecond; you don't want to repeat the same mistake

    d. Slap yourself silly for thinking of it and remember all of negative qualities your ex possesses

8. If you could quantify the qualities you value in a friend, for instance, loyalty and trust, you'd find that your ex possesses:

    a. Some of them

    b. All of them

    c. Most of them

    d. None of them

9. At this point, do you feel there are unresolved issues between you and your ex?

    a. Not really—at least not any that would hinder a friendship between us

    b. There are many such issues and we couldn't be friends unless we settled them

    c. Yes and we will never be able to get through them and have any real friendship

    d. There are some, but if we can work through them, we can probably be good friends

10. If your ex called you up to confide in you that s/he has been experiencing some difficult times, you would:

    a. Feel pleased that everyone has some rain in their lives

    b. Offer support and genuine empathy

    c. Tell your ex that you're not her/his therapist and hang up

    d. Wonder what your ex's motives are in telling you her/his problems, but would try to offer some advice

Scoring:

1. a = 1; b = 2; c = 3; d = 1	6. a = 2; b = 1; c = 3; d = 1
2. a = 3; b = 2; c = 1; d = 2	7. a = 3; b = 1; c = 1; d = 2
3. a = 1; b = 1; c = 3; d = 2	8. a = 2; b = 1; c = 2; d = 3
4. a = 1; b = 2; c = 3; d = 3	9. a = 3; b = 2; c = 1; d = 3
5. a = 3; b = 2; c = 1; d = 3; e = 2	10. a = 1; b = 3; c = 1; d = 2

● What Your Score Means

10 to 16:
You Are Definitely Not Ready to Become Friends with Your Ex

At this point, you need to listen to a lot of love songs and work through any anger you may be experiencing about your relationship and its demise. If you can resolve hurtful issues with your ex, it may be possible at some point to reestablish a friendly relationship. Right now, however, focus on healing yourself.

17 to 23:
Friendship with Your Ex Is a Maybe

You are at that stage where you may be able to be friends with your ex, but need motivation to carry on that type of relationship. Perhaps some unresolved feelings could account for your inertia. If you want to become friends with your ex, see if you can talk your feelings out. Invite your ex out for coffee sometime and see what develops from there. If you make the effort and nothing results from it, at least you won't feel like you're missing out on anything.

24 to 30:

You Can Be Friends with Your Ex

You seem to have ended the relationship on good terms, which helps in the development of a platonic relationship. Despite what romantic feelings you may have experienced for your ex, you can look past them now to consider more of a companionable relationship. You understand that even if the romance didn't work out the friendship can endure.

Can You Live without a Significant Other?

1. How often have you been without a significant other?

 a. Never

 b. Rarely

 c. Sometimes

 d. Frequently

 e. Always

2. You're going to be with your family for Thanksgiving dinner. You find yourself without a date. You are most likely to:

 a. Make an excuse to stay home so you don't have to go alone

 b. Feel upset about it but go anyway

 c. Bring a friend so you don't have to go alone

 d. Think nothing of it; you're proud to be on your own

3. When a serious relationship ends, how long before you start thinking of dating again?

 a. One week

 b. One month

 c. Six months

 d. One year

 e. Can't really say—when it's time, you'll know it

 f. As long as it takes to feel you're really over the old relationship

4. You've been invited to a party but your significant other can't go. You:

    a. Stay at home

    b. Go for a little while just to make an appearance

    c. Go and have a nice time on your own

    d. Are relieved. You would rather not be weighed down by a date

5. Your significant other has to go on a three-day business trip. It's your first time apart. You:

    a. Call every hour and send "just thinking of you" emails the entire time

    b. Check in to make sure all is well and go on with life

    c. Enjoy having some extra time to yourself

    d. Try to get time off from work so you can join your honey

6. You've been without a serious relationship for two months. You:

    a. Can't stand it and ask everyone you know to fix you up

    b. Figure that you'll meet someone, when it's the right time

    c. Enjoy the freedom and use the time to catch up with old friends

    d. Hit the singles scene hard until you find someone

7. You go out for dinner by yourself:

    a. Never!

    b. Occasionally

c. You don't have a problem going out alone but if you didn't have plans you'd probably just cook or bring in dinner

d. Frequently

8. Your dream mate ends your relationship. You:

a. Beg for a second chance

b. Figure it's all for the best and move on

c. Throw away all sentimental items from the relationship and never look back

d. Think about your ex all the time and do whatever you can to restart the romance

9. You're offered your dream job in a distant locale and you really want to move. The person you're dating has no desire to go. You:

a. Accept the job and break up

b. Pass up the job

c. Make things work long distance until you meet someone new

d. Make things work long distance because you want the relationship and the job

10. Your significant other wants to talk about some problems in your relationship. Your attitude is:

a. You'll do whatever is needed to make things better

b. You're open to improving the relationship as long as you both like the changes discussed

c. You know that you're not going to change so your partner has to love you as you are

d. You will do whatever you can to keep things going at least until you meet someone to take your partner's place

Scoring:

1. a = 3; b = 3; c = 2; d = 1; e = 1	**6.** a = 3; b = 2; c = 1; d = 3
2. a = 3; b = 2; c = 3; d = 1	**7.** a = 3; b = 2; c = 2; d = 1
3. a = 3; b = 3; c = 2; d = 1; e = 2; f = 1	**8.** a = 3; b = 2; c = 1; d = 3
4. a = 3; b = 2; c = 1; d = 1	**9.** a = 1; b = 3; c = 3; d = 2
5. a = 3; b = 2; c = 1; d = 3	**10.** a = 3; b = 2; c = 1; d = 3

● What Your Score Means

10 to 16:

Independent and Happy on Your Own

"Free and easy" is your motto. You are perfectly fine without a relationship. You go to movies alone, on trips alone and are happy to live life alone—you're a strong-willed independent person. It's great that you're confident and independent, but keep in mind that everyone needs other people sometimes and there is nothing wrong with that. Make sure that you're not sending signals that say you're so happy alone that you always want to be that way. A balance between independence and supportive relationships is the best combination.

17 to 23:

Slow and Steady

You've found the balance between having close relationships and maintaining your independence. You're comfortable facing the world as a single person or with a significant other by your side. While it can be difficult to endure long periods without dating someone you like, you find the positive aspects of being single— whether it's more time for yourself, your friends, your family or your career, you make the most of it. Keep up the good work!

24 to 30:
Relationship Needy

You're not sure that you can survive without a significant other—how would you know? You've hardly given yourself a chance to experience life on your own. If you had your way, you'd have a date every night. The only problem is that you don't know what it's like to be on your own. You stand by your partner, in front of your partner and behind your partner and forget to stand alone sometimes. Having fun in relationships is fine; just don't lose yourself along the way. Explore life on your own and you'll see that you don't need a relationship to make you happy.

Compatibility

The hardest relationship question of all comes down to the basic issue of whether or not you're right for one another. No relationship is perfect, but then again you never want to settle for second best. Can one survey tell you if this is the right person for you? Probably not . . . but by the time you've gone through most of the surveys in this section, you'll have an idea if this one is worth the effort.

Are You Right for Each Other?

1. How often do you argue?

   a. It feels like always

   b. Frequently

   c. Sometimes

   d. Rarely

   e. It seems like never

2. How would you classify your arguments?

   a. Intense. Lots of yelling and name-calling

   b. Emotional. You both get deeply involved, but it is usually for the best

   c. Constructive. You air out important issues

   d. Meaningless. You fight over silly things and don't take the arguments seriously

3. Why do you argue?

   a. For various reasons

   b. Only over important stuff

   c. Over lots of little things

   d. We find a different reason every day

4. If work or other responsibilities kept you from spending quality time with your partner for two weeks, would you be:

    a. Happy to have some time apart

    b. Indifferent

    b. Upset

    c. Very upset

    d. Devastated

5. When your mate asks you to spend a meal with his/her family, are you:

    a. Desperate to think of an excuse to get out of it

    b. Willing to go although you would rather not

    c. Excited

    d. It all depends on your mood

6. How often do you have sexual fantasies about other people?

    a. All the time

    b. Frequently

    c. Sometimes

    d. Rarely

    e. Never

7. When you picture your life twenty years from now do you imagine yourself:

    a. Working hard at your career, but your personal life is fuzzy

b. Living with your sweetie in your dream house

c. You have no idea what you will be doing

d. You don't know where you'll be, but your honey is by your side!

8. Has your partner ever cheated on you?

a. No

b. Not that you know of, but who can be sure?

c. You think so, but who can be sure?

d. Yes

e. Yes, but you've discussed it and you know it won't happen again

9. How would you describe the level of trust between the two of you?

a. Ironclad

b. Despite the occasional moments of doubt, pretty strong

c. Ok

d. Pretty weak

10. When you drift off to sleep each night, you think about:

a. Whether or not you want to get married

b. Your next vacation

c. Your partner

d. Someone other than your honey

e. It varies

Scoring:

1. a = 3; b = 3; c = 2; d = 1; e = 1   6. a = 3; b = 3; c = 2; d = 1; e = 1

2. a = 3; b = 2; c = 1; d = 2   7. a = 2; b = 1; c = 3; d = 1

3. a = 2; b = 1; c = 3; d = 3   8. a = 1; b = 2; c = 3; d = 3; e = 2

4. a = 3; b = 3; c = 2; d = 1; e = 1   9. a = 1; b = 2; c = 2; d = 3

5. a = 3; b = 2; c = 1; d = 2   10. a = 2; b = 2; c = 1; d = 3; e = 2

• What Your Score Means

10 to 16:

You Two Are Lovebirds

You don't have to worry whether you two are going to make it; your biggest concern is where to go on your honeymoon. It's a great feeling to instinctively know you're with the right person; just be sure not to take it for granted. Nothing has pulled apart more good couples than complacency, so keep an eye open for it. Keep it fun and keep appreciating it and who knows, maybe you two will even agree on the china pattern.

17 to 23:

You Two Are a Work in Progress

Healthy and successful relationships take a lot of work. You need to spend some time thinking—and talking—about what each of you wants out of the relationship and whether you are right for one another. While it's easy to rationalize things one way or the other, remember that your instincts are usually a great indicator of how you truly feel. But just because it may take a lot of time and effort to make the relationship work doesn't mean it's not worth struggling for. After all, the best things in life rarely come easily.

24 to 30:

You Are on Your Way to Splitsville

Although you may value much of what your partner has to offer, it is clear that some of your needs are unfulfilled. While you like or even love some things about your mate, are these positive qualities worth tolerating all the negative ones? Not every relationship has to lead to marriage, minivans and picket fences, but it is a good idea to have a strong foundation of love and respect along with some sense of the future when you are involved in a serious relationship. Because the fundamentals seem to be missing in this relationship, it's probably time to think about moving on. It is hard to start over, but once you do, you'll be a lot happier.

Are You Committed to Your Relationship?

1. Given the opportunity, would you ever cheat on your partner if there was no chance that they'd find out about it?

    a. Yes, definitely

    b. Maybe

    c. Not likely

    d. Never

2. How do you picture your relationship with your partner five years from now?

    a. It will be as good as, or even better than, it is now

    b. You wouldn't be surprised if you were no longer together

    c. You could see yourself still together, but who really knows what will happen in the future

    d. You take things day-by-day and don't think too much about the future

3. How do you feel about breaking up?

    a. "Breaking up" is not in your vocabulary

    b. It should be used as a last resort after all other avenues have been exhausted

    c. It is the best option for two people who are unhappy in their relationship

    d. It would be sad, but there are other fish in the sea

4. What do you do when you are unhappy about an issue in your relationship?

    a. Talk to your partner about it

    b. Keep it to yourself

    c. Fight with your partner about it

    d. Take all necessary measures (e.g., counseling) to resolve the issue

5. If you could go back in time to before you started dating, would you still want to do everything over and be with this person?

    a. Yes, definitely

    b. Probably

    c. Probably not

    d. Definitely not

6. How would you feel to be single again?

    a. Wonderful—it would be very liberating for you

    b. Ok—if you had to be single again, you'd deal with it

    c. Not sure—you wouldn't know unless it happened

    d. Not good—it would be very lonely

    e. Terrible—you would miss your partner too much

7. Do you ever wish that you were single?

    a. All the time

    b. Occasionally

    c. Rarely

    d. Never

8. What is the main reason you are together right now?

    a. Because you are deeply in love with your partner

    b. Because even though your relationship is not perfect, you're trying to solve the problems

    c. Because you don't want to be single

    d. Because you are afraid of what others would think of you if you split up

    e. None of these

9. How does the thought of seeing your partner day-in and day-out for the rest of your life make you feel?

    a. Absolutely wonderful

    b. Really great

    c. Pretty good

    d. Somewhat troubling

    e. Awful

10. How often do you think about having an affair?

    a. Often

    b. Rarely or never

    c. Occasionally—but would never actually have one

    d. You are currently having an affair or have had one

11. If your partner admitted to cheating on you, what would you do?

    a. End the relationship

    b. Stay together and go to couples' counseling

c. Separate and go to couples' counseling to try to resolve things

d. Trust that your partner is really sorry and would never do it again

e. Cheat on your partner, to get even

Scoring:

1. a = 1; b = 2; c = 3; d = 3

2. a = 3; b = 1; c = 2; d = 2

3. a = 3; b = 2; c = 2; d = 1

4. a = 2; b = 1; c = 1; d = 3

5. a = 3; b = 2; c = 1; d = 1

6. a = 1; b = 1; c = 2; d = 2; e = 3

7. a = 1; b = 1; c = 2; d = 3

8. a = 3; b = 2; c = 1; d = 1; e = 2

9. a = 3; b = 3; c = 2; d = 1; e = 1

10. a = 1; b = 3; c = 2; d = 1

11. a = 1; b = 3; c = 2; d = 3; e = 1

• What Your Score Means

11 to 16:
You Are Not Very Committed

It appears that you are thinking twice about this relationship and if it's right for you. There are several issues that have gone unresolved, and as a result, you feel distanced from your partner. You may have watched many of your friends and family members go through a breakup, and may be considering this as a solution. Perhaps it is time to sit down with your partner and have a serious discussion about your future together. Don't be afraid to seek professional help; many relationships can be turned around when communication gaps are bridged. Good luck!

17 to 22:

You Are Somewhat Committed

You enjoy the security of being in a couple, and would really like for your relationship to work. However, at times it seems as if there are too many roadblocks in the way of harmony. When problems arise, you and your partner tend to avoid tackling the issues. Instead, your frustrations are frequently expressed in other ways that are less pragmatic and only serve to divide the two of you. There are many qualities that you love about your mate—try to remember them during the difficult times. Work on opening up the lines of communication with your partner. Once you understand each other, problems will be easier to resolve.

23 to 28:

You Are Quite Committed

You feel very strongly about making your relationship succeed, and try your best to communicate with your partner about issues that arise. Most of the time, you are content. However, like most relationships, there are times when you question whether you can really stay with your partner. There are so many qualities that you love about each other, and you really want this person to be happy. During the difficult periods in your relationship, take the time to reflect on what each of you could do to bring the two of you closer together; any positive change is a step toward deeper intimacy.

29 to 33:

You Are Very Committed

Congratulations! You look like you will be able to stick by your mate's side for the long haul. You are willing to do whatever it takes to make your relationship work. You take a proactive approach to keeping your relationship strong, and when trouble does arise, you work hard to resolve the problems. You are not just in love with the idea of being in a couple—you are in love with your partner as a person, and would do anything to make your relationship succeed. You have set yourself up for a long and happy coexistence—keep up the good work!

Do You Trust Your Partner?

1. You're picking your significant other up at work and as you approach you find your partner talking with an attractive colleague. You:

    a. Wait patiently until the conversation ends

    b. Walk up and introduce yourself and make it clear that you're a couple

    c. Ask about it later

    d. Accuse your partner of flirting

2. When your partner makes plans to go out with friends, you usually:

    a. Do your own thing and hope you both have a great time

    b. Go to the same place with your friends that night to keep an eye on your partner

    c. Ask if you can come along

    d. Make a comment about it being ok to look, but not to touch

3. When you think about your ex, you remember that:

    a. S/he cheated on you

    b. You couldn't trust her/him

    c. S/he couldn't trust you

    d. S/he lied occasionally

    e. You cared for one another

4. You're walking with your partner and a good-looking person passes and gives your mate a suggestive look. You:

    a. Elbow your partner

    b. Watch to see if your partner returns the stranger's look

    c. Comment on how attractive the person is and forget it

    d. Look around for a cute person of your own to check out

5. If your partner forgets to call you, you:

    a. Are suspicious

    b. Call your partner

    c. Don't notice

    d. Go find your partner

6. After a night out with friends, your partner gets in very late. You:

    a. Are not even home yet

    b. Are sound asleep

    c. Get mad

    d. Are out looking for your partner

    e. Ask your partner where s/he was all night

7. Your partner is two hours late—and you have tickets to a show that you know s/he didn't really want to go to. S/he tells you an in-depth story explaining the late arrival. You:

    a. Accuse him/her of being late on purpose

    b. Are suspicious, but accept the story

c. Believe the story

d. Are upset you missed the show, but know it's no one's fault

8. If you saw someone making moves on your partner, you would:

a. Make threats

b. Be amused

c. Accuse your partner of flirting

d. Ask what happened

9. How often do you accuse your partner of lying?

a. Never

b. Sometimes

c. Often

d. Always

10. A business trip means that you and your partner are in separate cities for a week. You:

a. Ask a friend to check up on your partner to keep tabs on what's going on while you're away

b. Talk to your partner about your fears that s/he may cheat while you're gone

c. Recognize that it would be easy for your partner to cheat but try not to think about

d. Feel confident that your partner will be faithful while you're out of town

Scoring:

1. a = 1; b = 3; c = 2; d = 3	6. a = 1; b = 1; c = 3; d = 3; e = 2
2. a = 1; b = 3; c = 3; d = 2	7. a = 3; b = 2; c = 1; d = 1
3. a = 3; b = 3; c = 1; d = 2	8. a = 3; b = 1; c = 3; d = 2
4. a = 2; b = 3; c = 1; d = 2; e = 1	9. a = 1; b = 2; c = 3; d = 3
5. a = 3; b = 2; c = 1; d = 3	10. a = 3; b = 2; c = 2; d = 1

● What Your Score Means

10 to 16:
You Have 100 Percent Trust

You clearly trust your partner and don't worry about being cheated on. If your significant other has worked hard to gain your complete trust and totally deserves it, your relationship seems to be going in a great direction. Have you ever thought about why you trust your partner as much as you do? If you have good reason, then congratulations! You've found a winner! Just be sure that your partner deserves all of this trust so that you can give it with confidence and conviction.

17 to 23:
Your Trust Is Shaky

Overall, you seem to trust your significant other. However, you sometimes like to check up to be sure your partner is being truthful. If your relationship is still young, this is fairly normal. After all, you don't want to be blindly trusting, since trust is something that needs to be earned. However, if you two have been together for a long time, this may be problematic. Perhaps you have been burned in the past and are having problems trusting again. Whatever the reason, you should think about this, because your bouts of distrust may push your partner away. After all, trust is a basic foundation of a good relationship.

24 to 30:
No Trust Here

You clearly do not trust your significant other, and you are constantly on guard. This may be due to your partner's attitude, behavior or past actions. If this is the case, you need to think about whether or not you really want to be with someone you can't trust. However, if there is no logical reason for your distrustful attitude, you should figure out where your feelings are coming from. Perhaps you feel insecure, or you may have been betrayed in past relationships. If this is the case, then you are not treating your partner— or yourself—fairly. Trust is an important foundation of every relationship, and if yours is shaky, you need to figure out why.

Does Your Partner Trust You?

1. You have a late Saturday night out with friends. When you get in super late, your partner:

  a. Is not home yet

  b. Is sound asleep

  c. Gets mad

  d. Is out looking for you

  e. Asks where you've been

2. Your partner hears a sexy voice leaving a message on your machine and:

  a. Asks who it is

  b. Dials *69 to find out who it was

  c. Does nothing

  d. Assumes you're cheating

3. Your friends want you to go clubbing Friday night, so you ask your sweetie if it's ok. Your partner:

  a. Tells you to have fun

  b. Goes to the same club to keep an eye on you

  c. Asks if s/he can come along

  d. Reminds you to look, but not touch

4. A good-looking person gives you a suggestive look as you pass by on the street. Your partner:

    a. Elbows you to remind you that you have a partner

    b. Accuses you of staring at the hottie

    c. Agrees that the person is hot and forgets it

    d. Is busy checking out the hottie's partner

5. Your partner picks you up at your office and finds you talking to an attractive colleague. Your partner:

    a. Waits patiently until you finish your conversation

    b. Walks up and makes it clear that you're a couple

    c. Asks you about it later

    d. Accuses you of flirting

6. If you forget to call your partner, your partner:

    a. Is suspicious

    b. Calls you

    c. Doesn't notice

    d. Tracks you down

7. If someone hit on you, your partner would:

    a. Make threats

    b. Be amused

    c. Accuse you of flirting

    d. Ask you what happened

8. Your car breaks down and you arrive two hours late for a date to see a concert. Your partner knows that you didn't really want to go. S/he:

   a. Accuses you of being late on purpose

   b. Is suspicious, but accepts your story

   c. Believes you

   d. Is sad that you missed the show, but doesn't blame you

9. How often do you and your partner discuss trust issues?

   a. Never

   b. Sometimes

   c. Often

   d. Always

10. How often does your sweetie accuse you of lying?

   a. Never

   b. Sometimes

   c. Often

   d. Always

Scoring:

1. a = 1; b = 1; c = 3; d = 3; e = 2	**6.** a = 3; b = 2; c = 1; d = 3
2. a = 2; b = 3; c = 1; d = 3	**7.** a = 3; b = 1; c = 3; d = 2
3. a = 1; b = 3; c = 3; d = 2	**8.** a = 3; b = 2; c = 1; d = 1
4. a = 2; b = 3; c = 1; d = 1	**9.** a = 1; b = 2; c = 3; d = 3
5. a = 1; b = 3; c = 2; d = 3	**10.** a = 1; b = 2; c = 3; d = 3

• What Your Score Means

10 to 16:
Your Partner Has Complete Trust in You

Congratulations—your significant other trusts you implicitly. If you have proved yourself trustworthy, then you two are on the right track. Having faith in a relationship is impossible if you don't trust your partner. If you have not been together for very long, however, then it may seem that your partner doesn't care what you may be doing when you're apart. If this concerns you, then talk about it. Trust is one of the most important ingredients in a healthy relationship, and knowing that your partner will open up to you about important feelings is a big part of trusting someone. Good luck!

17 to 23:
Your Partner Has Some Doubts about Your Trustworthiness

Overall, your significant other seems to trust you. However, sometimes there is an urge to check up on you to see whether the trust is validated. If you two are at the beginning of a relationship, this is fairly normal, since trust is something that is usually earned. However, if you two have been together for a really long time, then a problem might exist. If this concerns you, then talk about it. Trust is one of the most fundamental components in a lasting relationship, and knowing that your partner will discuss the issues involved in commitment is a critical aspect of trusting someone. Good luck!

24 to 30:
No Trust Here

Your significant other seems to be mistrustful of you. There is a constant fear of betrayal, which may be due to something that happened between the two of you. If this is the case, then you need to do some work to earn back the trust. If you have been completely honest, though, the reluctance to trust might be coming from something that someone else did. If this concerns you, then talk about it. That's very important, because trust is one of the most crucial aspects of a strong relationship. You need to be able to communicate openly in order to really trust and be trusted. Good luck!

Are You Ready to Move in Together?

1. You want to move in together because:

    a. You love each other

    b. Your partner is pressuring you to move in together

    c. You want to spend as much time together as possible

    d. All your friends are living with people or married

    e. Why pay rent on two places when you're always together anyway?

2. What will you do when you want to go out and your partner wants to stay in?

    a. Go out—you aren't joined at the hip

    b. Stay in—going out isn't that important to you

    c. Go out after you have spent time together

    d. Fight about it

    e. Discuss it

3. The best part of moving in together is:

    a. Spending more time together

    b. Firming up your commitment

    c. Learning about each other

    d. Postponing marriage

4. Your friend sees your partner at a suspicious "meeting" with a member of the opposite sex. You:

   a. Assume it was a legitimate meeting

   b. Conclude that your partner is cheating on you

   c. Ask your partner for all the details

   d. Figure that your friend is mistaken and forget it

5. When it comes to financial matters, your partner:

   a. Is very responsible

   b. Has never balanced a checkbook

   c. Doesn't have a job

   d. Can be trusted to handle half of the bills

6. When you discuss living together, your partner:

   a. Prefers not to discuss it

   b. Is happy to talk about it

   c. Is enthusiastic about moving forward

   d. Expresses some second thoughts

7. When you are living together, who will be responsible for chores?

   a. You

   b. Your partner

   c. You will split the work

   d. You haven't discussed it

   e. You've agreed to hire a maid service

8. When you tell your friends that you and your partner might be moving in together, they'll probably say:

a. "Congratulations!"

b. "Already?"

c. "Oh no, not another one."

d. "When can we come for dinner?"

9. When you look at your partner, you think:

a. "How did I get so lucky?"

b. "Do I really know this person?"

c. "I hope this works out."

d. "What am I doing?"

10. Your main fear is that:

a. You're not ready for such a big change

b. Your partner will leave dirty socks on the floor

c. Your partner doesn't want this as much as you do

d. If you break up, it will be that much harder because you live together

Scoring:

1. a = 3; b = 1; c = 2; d = 1; e = 1	**6.** a = 1; b = 2; c = 3; d = 1
2. a = 2; b = 2; c = 3; d = 1; e = 3	**7.** a = 1; b = 1; c = 3; d = 2; e = 3
3. a = 3; b = 2; c = 3; d = 1	**8.** a = 3; b = 2; c = 1; d = 3
4. a = 3; b = 1; c = 2; d = 3	**9.** a = 3; b = 1; c = 2; d = 1
5. a = 3; b = 1; c = 1; d = 2	**10.** a = 2; b = 3; c = 1; d = 1

• What Your Score Means

10 to 16:
You Should Keep Your Own Place

You say you want to move in together, but are you really ready for this? Living with someone is an important step and one that should not be taken based on financial needs or a fear of being alone. Don't move in together so you can keep a closer eye on your partner or push the relationship to a place it hasn't evolved to yet. If your relationship lacks a strong base, sharing a home is not necessarily the way to firm up your foundation. Relationship work needs to be done before, not after, you start splitting the rent. Look before you leap!

17 to 23:
You Need to Think Things Through

At this point in your relationship, moving in together may or may not be the best idea. You need to consider the stage of your relationship, and where you want it to go. Is your partner someone that you trust and care for, or a warm body to sleep next to and a way to reduce your rent? If your relationship lacks a strong base, sharing an apartment is not necessarily the way to strengthen your connection. If you two are really meant for one another, though, put aside your hesitations and forge ahead, but be prepared to put in some time learning to negotiate each other's boundaries. Good luck!

24 to 30:
Cohabitation, Here You Come!

You know you love your partner and recognize that it's time to take the relationship to the next level. You are tired of dashing home in the morning to change your socks and underwear before work and want your lover's toothbrush to have a permanent home near yours. Living together means intensifying your commitment to one another, so make sure you discuss the issues that might come up and establish solutions that will work for both of you. That way you won't be left arguing about whose turn it is to wash the dishes, and instead, you'll be able to concentrate on romance. Congratulations!

Are You and Your Partner Sexually Compatible?

1. Your kissing styles are:

   a. Totally opposite

   b. Just fine; you never really noticed

   c. Exactly the same

   d. Different, but marvelous together nonetheless

2. After sexual activities, you and your partner usually:

   a. Spoon

   b. Go your separate ways

   c. Fight over the good side of the bed

   d. Caress till it's time to go at it again

3. When you initiate sexual activities, your partner:

   a. Always wants it, too

   b. Usually is up for it

   c. Frequently turns you away

   d. Occasionally declines

4. In terms of making noise during sexual activities, if your partner gets loud, you:

   a. Are too busy to notice

b. Love it

c. Are bothered by it

d. Enjoy it

5. You're at the movies when your partner slides a hand down your pants. Do you:

a. Reciprocate

b. Stop your partner

c. Giggle and go with it

d. Ask your partner to save it for later

6. Variety-wise, the two of you:

a. Rely on one or two positions

b. Experiment constantly

c. Try something new every once in a while

d. Change quite a bit, depending on your moods

7. When it comes to personal hygiene, your partner:

a. Doesn't shower enough for you

b. Is a model of cleanliness

c. Could use a few more swipes of the razor

d. Smells (and tastes) great

8. The most important thing during sexual activities is:

a. Your partner's pleasure

b. Your pleasure

c. That you both have pleasure

d. That you both feel comfortable

9. The sight of your partner's face during sexual pleasure:

a. Distracts you

b. Is wonderful

c. Surprises you

d. Is weird

e. Freaks you out

Scoring:

1. a = 3; b = 2; c = 1; d = 2

2. a = 2; b = 3; c = 3; d = 1

3. a = 1; b = 2; c = 3; d = 2

4. a = 2; b = 1; c = 3; d = 1

5. a = 1; b = 3; c = 1; d = 2

6. a = 3; b = 1; c = 2; d = 1

7. a = 3; b = 1; c = 2; d = 1

8. a = 3; b = 3; c = 1; d = 2

9. a = 3; b = 1; c = 2; d = 3; e = 3

● What Your Score Means

9 to 14:

Sexual Soul Mates

You and your partner sure know how to get it on; being affectionate is something you do very well together. Considerate of each other's needs and desires, you both ensure that the other has a pleasurable experience every time you come together. Your attraction for each other is strong, and every experience you share makes it that much more passionate. Compatible? You bet—you two are denizens of desire.

15 to 21
Easygoing Ecstasy

While you and your partner may not see eye-to-eye on every aspect of your sexual relationship, you've found more than enough similarities to keep things hopping. Sometimes there's a bit of conflict, but your mutual lust and consideration tend to take care of any potential tussles. Generally, you get along just fine when you're getting intimate, and when there is a desire difference, you find a way to make it work. You two have managed to merge your sexual tastes into a relationship that satisfies you both.

22 to 27
I Say Cuddly, You Say Kinky

Sometimes you can utterly adore someone, but the chemistry doesn't automatically carry into the bedroom. In the case of you and your partner, sexual activities of late have not been as great as you deserve. Regardless, just because your sexual styles are different does not mean that you aren't good for each other or that you can't make things better. Recognizing that you have room to improve could lead you to better ways of turning each other on; enhancing your sex life could be one of the most exciting learning experiences you've ever had—when it comes to improving your sexual relationship, practice makes perfect!

Are You in Love or in Lust?

1. You were first attracted to your partner's:

   a. Personality

   b. Physical appearance

   c. Willingness to have a physical relationship

   d. Sense of humor

2. About how often do thoughts of a sexual nature enter your mind when you're with your partner?

   a. Every hour

   b. About once a day

   c. Every now and then

   d. Incessantly

3. If necessary, how long do you think you could go without having a physical relationship with your partner?

   a. A week

   b. A month

   c. An hour or two

   d. A day

4. A typical date with your partner consists primarily of:

   a. Going to dinner and a movie

b. Intimate activities

c. Doing any activity so you can work up a sweat for later

d. Doing something you mutually enjoy

5. When you and your partner are walking together, you often find that you are:

a. Holding each other's hand

b. Groping and grinding with each other

c. Arm-in-arm

d. Side by side—not touching

6. When you express your feelings for your partner, you often find yourself saying something like:

a. "I want you."

b. "I love you."

c. "I need you."

d. "I adore you."

7. If your partner suddenly couldn't fulfill your sexual needs (because of an injury, business trip or other unavoidable reason), how long would you remain in the relationship?

a. As long as it took to find someone new

b. Indefinitely; there's more to our relationship than just a physical intimacy

c. A little while, out of guilt and a sense of duty to my partner

d. I might be forced to cheat a little bit but would try to save the relationship

8. Your partner and your parents are:

    a. Getting together next week for the first time; you're excited about it and hope it goes well

    b. Never ever going to meet. You're not with the type of person you'd want to bring home to Mom and Dad

    c. Planning to get together soon, since they had so much fun the last time you all spent time together

    d. Getting along great, especially since they've met several times

9. How long do you think this relationship will last?

    a. Hopefully forever

    b. Until the physical intimacy dwindles

    c. Until it becomes stagnant

    d. Until we have our first huge fight

10. Your friends think your partner:

    a. Is perfect for you. They've met your partner several times and get along great

    b. Doesn't exist. They've never met your partner because you two are too busy

    c. Is a good person, based on the impression they formed during the one time they met

    d. Is compatible with you physically, but doesn't share much else in common with you

11. When you see your partner, the first thing you want to do is:

    a. Get in bed together

    b. Give your partner a hug and a kiss

c. Say hello

d. Ask your partner how his/her day was

Scoring:

1. a = 2; b = 3; c = 3; d = 1	**7.** a = 3; b = 1; c = 2; d = 3
2. a = 3; b = 2; c = 1; d = 3	**8.** a = 2; b = 3; c = 1; d = 1
3. a = 1; b = 1; c = 3; d = 2	**9.** a = 1; b = 3; c = 1; d = 2
4. a = 2; b = 3; c = 3; d = 1	**10.** a = 1; b = 2; c = 2; d = 3
5. a = 2; b = 3; c = 2; d = 1	**11.** a = 3; b = 2; c = 1; d = 1
6. a = 3; b = 1; c = 2; d = 1	

● What Your Score Means

11 to 16:

More Love Than Lust

Your answers indicate that your relationship is governed more by love than by lust. This is not to say that it is a platonic, asexual relationship. There definitely is a physical intimacy present in the relationship, but it doesn't dominate it. Having a loving relationship, as opposed to one that is more heavily based on physical needs, is healthier for both partners and will develop more deeply and last much longer.

17 to 22:

A Little More Love Than Lust

On the love/lust continuum, you and your partner are leaning more in the direction of a loving relationship. This is great, since it's better in the long run to develop a relationship based on friendship and love first before adding a physical component to the mix. You can always work on developing physical intimacy as you grow together.

23 to 28:
A Little More Lust Than Love

Although you and your partner do engage in other activities together, you have a relationship that is predominantly physical in nature. If you're satisfied with this type of relationship, that's fine, but if you want to form a bond on another level, you should start discovering and developing new interests together. What do you and your partner have in common beyond the bedroom? Begin your evaluation of your relationship by engaging in a dialogue with your partner and take it from there.

29 to 33:
Lust Rules

All signs point to a common theme in your relationship with your partner: lust. The relationship is controlled by physical cravings. While it's great to have a strong attraction for your partner, you may want to explore your relationship to determine if you have any other sentiments beyond the physical. Lust is a particularly volatile feeling. If it disappears, you'll be left high and dry with a relationship void that cannot be filled.

Is Your Partner Marriage Material?

1. When it comes to discussing commitment, your partner:

   a. Loves to talk about your future together

   b. Doesn't like the thought of being "tied down"

   c. Will discuss it if you bring it up

   d. Loves to change the subject

2. How does your partner view the future?

   a. Actively saving for retirement

   b. Can't plan beyond this weekend

   c. Making career plans that allow for family time

   d. Talks about investing at a later date but does not focus on it right now

3. On your birthday, your partner:

   a. Does nothing

   b. Buys a thoughtful gift

   c. Buys you something if reminded by a friend or family member (or you)

   d. Takes you somewhere special

4. Your sex life is:

   a. Ok

b. Loving and satisfying

c. Exciting and fun

d. Needs improvement

5. When you talk about sex, your partner is:

   a. Open, curious and attentive

   b. Rather uncomfortable but tries to open up

   c. Unwilling to discuss it

   d. Selfish—trying to coach you without asking for any pointers

6. When you talk about your career, your partner:

   a. Is interested and supportive

   b. Seems uninterested

   c. Pressures you to work more or less than you would like

   d. Is supportive, but does not take your career seriously

7. Your partner's family is:

   a. Distant

   b. Welcoming

   c. Neutral

   d. Quirky

8. Your partner's current status is:

   a. Committed to you 100 percent

   b. Dating you and a few other people and loving it

   c. Dating you exclusively for a few months

d. Broke up with someone else recently but is very interested in you

9. When you disagree, your partner:

   a. Sees arguments as a fight that someone has to "win"

   b. Gets completely enraged

   c. May get mad, but will always cool down and talk it out

   d. Looks for compromises and "win/win" solutions with you

10. When you two have plans, your partner:

   a. Is always late

   b. Sometimes cancels at the last minute

   c. Is on time and calls if s/he has been delayed

   d. Often changes plans at the last minute, without asking you

11. When your partner makes a promise, your partner:

   a. Always follows through

   b. Rarely follows through and makes many excuses

   c. Follows through but often needs a reminder

   d. Repeats the promise frequently, but never actually follows through

12. Your partner's sense of humor:

   a. Is hysterical

   b. Is great

   c. Can usually cheer you up

d. Is annoying

e. Embarrasses you

Scoring:

1. a = 3; b = 1; c = 2; d = 1	**7.** a = 1; b = 3; c = 2; d = 2
2. a = 3; b = 1; c = 3; d = 2	**8.** a = 3; b = 1; c = 3; d = 2
3. a = 1; b = 3; c = 2; d = 3	**9.** a = 1; b = 1; c = 2; d = 3
4. a = 2; b = 3; c = 3; d = 1	**10.** a = 2; b = 1; c = 3; d = 1
5. a = 3; b = 2; c = 1; d = 1	**11.** a = 3; b = 1; c = 2; d = 1
6. a = 3; b = 1; c = 1; d = 2	**12.** a = 3; b = 3; c = 2; d = 1; e = 1

● What Your Score Means

12 to 19:
You Need to Pass This One by

While you may be having fun for now, if you are looking for a long-term commitment, keep looking. Even if you really feel passionately about this partner you'll probably be better off getting back into the dating game. Your partner may not be ready to take the relationship to the next level, let alone to the altar. Are you really looking for permanence? If not, enjoy your mate for all the things that attract you. If you're set on wedding bells, get out there and starting looking for the real marriage material.

20 to 28:
You Have a Marriage, Maybe

This partner is a fixer-upper. There are some of the qualities that make a marriage work, but you might need to work on some others.

Consider setting aside a regular time to discuss your relationship and the progress that you're making on getting closer to one another. Before making a life-long commitment you need to make sure you can both communicate, problem solve and work as a team when the going gets rough. Remember that while you can improve the way you interact, it is impossible to change people. Think about what you really expect from each other and if you can both realistically meet those requirements. If so, then it's worth working to enhance the relationship. If you can't meet one another's needs, it's time to consider moving on.

29 to 36:
You've Found Marriage Material!

Sit your partner down and express how you feel because you've found a keeper! Marriage takes work, trust and communication, and your partner is clearly someone you can talk to. You will be able to work together to build a beautiful life. As a couple, you can work to take your relationship to the next level and eventually to the altar. These partners are rare, so treat this one like gold and you will get the same in return.

Working to Make Love Work

Once you've met the right person and have actually entered into a steady relationship, you may think you have accomplished a lot—and in the dating world you have! But you need to realize that the hardest part is yet to come: making your relationship work. While there are two sides to every story, you need to get your side straight so that you can communicate with your partner. Here is where you need to ask the tough questions: Are you too controlling? Is your partner insensitive to your needs? Can you trust each other? The first question is, should you take these surveys in private, with your mate or with your friends—it's all up to you.

Are You in Love?

1. When you think about you and your partner a year from now, you hear:

   a. Wedding bells

   b. The crack of a whip

   c. The din of the bar where you're picking up a new flame

   d. The sounds of laughter and good times

2. What "L" word best describes your feelings about your partner?

   a. "Love"—this is it!

   b. "Like"—you think you're on the right path together, but you're not 100 percent sure

   c. "Lust"—the chemistry is great, but what about the rest?

   d. "Light"—as in the light of your life

3. It's time to introduce your significant other to your parents. You:

   a. Are really nervous

   b. Are excited. You know they'll hit it off

   c. Instruct your sweetie on the best ways to please your parents

   d. Put it off as long as you possibly can

4. Six months into your relationship, your significant other gets a job offer that's in a city far away. This job is too good to pass up. You:

a. Are upset beyond words. How can your partner even think of leaving you for a job?

b. Follow your partner to the new city

c. Decide that you'll make the distance work—between the phone and the plane, you'll get together as often as you can

d. Deal with the situation in a cool manner. If things work out, great. If not, it was not meant to be

5. You've discovered some rather sordid details about your partner's dating past. You:

a. Pretend that there is no past

b. Break up

c. Address the issues openly. Open communication is essential to get through rough spots

d. Berate your partner and then try to overlook the past

6. After you and your partner have a major argument, you:

a. Forgive and forget

b. Leave the room in a huff and refuse to speak until you hear an apology

c. Realize that in a relationship, you're going to have arguments. It's what you do when you make up that counts

d. Insist that you were right, but realize that one argument should not impact the entire relationship

7. You've been stressed lately and you suspect your partner is beginning to think you're a grouch. When asked what's wrong, you:

a. Say nothing about your problems

b. Share your troubles. A relationship needs to include the good times and the bad ones

c. Try sharing some of your woes to see how your partner responds. If that goes well, you'll share the rest

d. Mention one thing that's bugging you and leave it at that

8. You're annoyed by the amount of time your partner spends on hobbies that don't interest you. You:

a. Ask if you could spend more time together doing things you both enjoy

b. Demand that your partner cut down on these activities

c. Try to learn to like your partner's hobbies

d. Complain to your friends. You don't want to change your partner, but you need to vent

9. How easily can you say those three little words (I love you!) and mean them?

a. As smooth as butter

b. Not without feeling sick

c. With butterflies in your stomach

d. You stammer a little when you try to get the words out

10. Which of the following quotations is most relevant to your feelings about love?

a. "If love is the answer, could you please rephrase the question?"—Lily Tomlin

b. "There is only one happiness in life, to love and be loved."—George Sand

c. "Love ceases to be a pleasure when it ceases to be a secret."
—Aphra Behn

d. "Love never dies of starvation, but often of indigestion."
—Anne de Lenclos

Scoring:

1. a = 3; b = 1; c = 1; d = 2

2. a = 3; b = 2; c = 1; d = 3

3. a = 2; b = 3; c = 2; d = 1

4. a = 2; b = 3; c = 3; d = 1

5. a = 2; b = 1; c = 3; d = 1

6. a = 3; b = 1; c = 3; d = 2

7. a = 1; b = 3; c = 2; d = 1

8. a = 3; b = 1; c = 3; d = 2

9. a = 3; b = 1; c = 2; d = 2

10. a = 1; b = 3; c = 2; d = 2

● What Your Score Means

10 to 16:

You Are Closer to Like Than Love

Maybe this relationship isn't the right one for you. It seems that you're not satisfied with your partner or that your feelings may have soured. Examine recent events in your relationship. Do the positive ones outweigh the negative ones? Is there more "give" than "take" on either side? Don't let one bad relationship color your perspective; even if you're unlucky in love once (or twice), you'll meet the right person when you're ready. In the meantime, you can work on mending your heart and preparing yourself for entering a great relationship.

17 to 23:

Listen to Your Heart

No one is perfect, but it sounds like this person may have seemed that way at one point. Once infatuation's blinders come off, you realize the flaws in the other person and the possible cracks in the relationship. When you love someone, you're not necessarily blind to the other person's faults; you may even grow to adore them. Additionally, your feelings need to come from within and should not need to be validated by anyone else—like your parents or friends. Can you weather storms in the relationship? If so, then you will be traveling in the love lane. Give it some more time to find out.

24 to 30:

Love Is in the Air

You're in a mutually satisfying relationship, one that brings you great joy and peace, as well as fulfillment. This is the gold standard for which people strive. There was a little bit of luck involved (i.e., meeting the right person), but to fully realize love, you must build the relationship slowly and work on it. Physical chemistry only gets you so far—the rest of it relies on your willingness to sort out problems and surmount obstacles together. Lucky you!

Are You Ready for Commitment?

1. You have a second date scheduled for Friday night, but a friend calls that day with last-minute tickets to a concert you've been wanting to see. You:

    a. Make up an excuse to cancel your date and go to the concert

    b. Be honest with your date when you call to reschedule and go to the concert but plan a special date for another night to make up for the last-minute change

    c. Skip the concert and keep the date

    d. Fit both into the plans—meet your date for drinks before or after the concert

2. It's your birthday. Your plans are:

    a. A candlelight dinner for two with your partner

    b. A night out for you and thirty of your friends

    c. Dinner with the friends and then meet up with your partner for drinks

    d. Two celebrations—one with a group and one alone with your mate

3. You've gone on a few dates and are considering being exclusive when a coworker offers to set you up with her cousin who promises to be gorgeous, successful and lots of fun. You:

    a. Say yes to the setup

    b. Decline the offer

c. Suggest she invite her cousin to happy hour after work

d. Decline the offer and discuss being exclusive with your new honey

4. You're invited to a family wedding and can bring a guest. You:

a. Invite a friend—you're not ready to introduce your new partner to the whole family

b. Go dateless—weddings can be great places to meet new people

c. Take your new mate—you're ready for the full-family encounter

d. Take your new mate—but mention that going together is not a big deal

5. On New Year's Eve, you plan to be:

a. Cuddling with your date and sipping champagne

b. At your friend's dinner party with ten other couples

c. Smooching with the hottest person you can find at a New Year's bash

d. You're not sure because you don't know if you'll be together

6. Your best friend has just called you about a recent crisis, but you're about to leave for a date with your new honey. You:

a. Cancel your date and go to your friend in need

b. Call to let your date know you'll be late and talk to your friend for fifteen minutes

c. Explain the situation to your date and postpone your date time for an hour

d. Tell your friend that you will call her as soon as you get home from your date

7. Your new mate makes plans for friends to come over to watch their favorite show—you're not a big fan. You:

    a. Stop by with some snacks or a bottle of wine

    b. Suggest inviting a few more people and making it a party together

    c. Make separate plans with friends

    d. Stop by for a little while but then head out to do your own thing

8. After having gone on five dates with a partner, how do you refer to this person when speaking to your coworkers?

    a. "The person I just started dating"

    b. "Partner" or "girlfriend" or "boyfriend"

    c. Why mention it all—you've only been out a few times

    d. "My newest love interest"

Scoring:

1. a = 1; b = 2; c = 3; d = 2	**5.** a = 3; b = 2; c = 1; d = 1
2. a = 3; b = 1; c = 2; d = 3	**6.** a = 1; b = 2; c = 3; d = 3
3. a = 1; b = 3; c = 2; d = 3	**7.** a = 3; b = 3; c = 1; d = 2
4. a = 2; b = 1; c = 3; d = 2	**8.** a = 2; b = 3; c = 1; d = 2

● What Your Score Means

8 to 11:
Not Ready to Commit

"The more fun the better" is your motto. You are too curious about new people to really settle down and commit to dating one special someone. No date, no matter how fabulous, has a chance of breaking into your world. You're having a blast, and that's great. Just make sure that you're not avoiding commitment for any deeper reasons. Also, shed the notion that commitment means your life has to get boring. Intimacy with one person could be just the excitement you crave.

12 to 15:
You Are Considering Commitment

Maybe you've been burned in the past or maybe you're just having a fun time with your friends. Whatever your reasons, you're not super anxious to jump into a serious relationship right now. But, if the right person comes along, you'd be willing to give it a shot, right? Good for you for keeping an open mind and trying to keep a steady balance in your life.

16 to 20:
You Are Ready for Commitment

You are ready to commit when the right person comes along. You're not afraid to leave the dating scene and put your faith in one special someone. Even though you're open to the idea of a steady relationship, you're not willing to be serious with any person who happens to come your way. You're waiting to find someone you really care for because you understand that relationships are challenging and a strong foundation is crucial for success.

21 to 24:

You Are Commitment Crazed!

Slow down! You're clearly ready to meet that special someone and commit to them ASAP. It's great to know what you want, but be careful—do you really dig that person or do you just want to fill that empty spot? You're so anxious to commit that you may scare your dates off with your forward style. Solid relationships are built upon a strong foundation of shared interests, mutual values and open communication. Take the time to get to know someone and your commitment will be a much more successful one.

How Far Would You Go for Love?

1. If your partner got a job across the country and had to relocate, you would probably:

    a. Quit your job and move together

    b. Think about moving in together

    c. Break up

    d. Try to make things work long distance

2. Your partner is away for the weekend and you're in a bar with friends when an attractive person smiles at you from across the room. You:

    a. Invite the person to join you and your group

    b. Start talking to the person and spend the entire evening together if you like each other

    c. Smile at the person but stay with your friends

    d. Get the person's number and return to your friends

    e. Ignore the person

3. You have plans with friends but your partner asks you to stay home instead. You:

    a. Reschedule with your friends

    b. Invite your friends over, too

    c. Go out with your friends

    d. Spend some time with your friends, then leave early to be with your honey

4. Your partner wants you to go away together on the same weekend that you were planning on taking a vacation with your family. You:

    a. Go with your partner

    b. Go with your family

    c. Spend part of the time with your partner and part with your family

    d. Plan it so you can all go away together

5. When it comes to love, your friends would probably say that you are:

    a. Willing to be with anyone who comes along

    b. Always looking for love

    c. A true romantic

    d. Very rational

    e. Not the lovey type

6. Your new boss is very attractive, and seems like he or she could be the one for you. For life. You:

    a. Do what you can to try to ignite a romance

    b. Maintain your professionalism and try to keep your distance

    c. Force yourself to forget the attraction because you disapprove of office romances

    d. Think about changing jobs so you can get going with the romance

7. Your partner dislikes your best friend. You:

    a. Break up with your partner

b. Stop seeing your friend

c. Maintain both relationships but keep them separate

d. Ask your partner to keep an open mind and explain all the good you see in your friend

8. You just got the job of your dreams—on the other side of the country. You:

a. Ask your partner to come with you

b. Decide not to go

c. Break up

d. Try to make things work long distance

9. The night of the concert you've been looking forward to for months, your partner comes down with the flu. You:

a. Stay home and nurse your honey back to health

b. Pack a bag of cold medicine and drag your partner to the concert

c. Go to the concert with a friend

d. Go to half of the concert and then come home and play nurse

e. Go to the concert if you can find someone else to come over and keep your partner company

10. Your partner has a meaningless kiss with an old flame and confesses to you right away. You:

a. Forgive and forget . . . eventually

b. Take time to think about it but give your partner a chance to regain your trust

c. Break up

d. Have your own "illegal" kiss and then call it even

Scoring:

1. a = 3; b = 2; c = 1; d = 1

2. a = 1; b = 2; c = 2; d = 2; e = 3

3. a = 3; b = 2; c = 1; d = 2

4. a = 3; b = 1; c = 2; d = 3

5. a = 1; b = 3; c = 3; d = 2; e = 1

6. a = 3; b = 1; c = 1; d = 3

7. a = 1; b = 3; c = 3; d = 2

8. a = 3; b = 3; c = 1; d = 2

9. a = 3; b = 2; c = 1; d = 2; e = 2

10. a = 3; b = 1; c = 2; d = 1

● What Your Score Means

10 to 16:

You're Not Ready to Go Very Far for Love

You are as interested in romance as the next person, but you aren't willing to give up your goals, plans, friends or ideals in order to get it. Realizing that a relationship is not the only thing in your life, you have figured out that you need a balance of many things. As important as your previous commitments are, though, sometimes the best things in life come as inconvenient surprises, and you've got to be ready to take a chance once in awhile. Meanwhile, your friends and family appreciate the attention you give them, and your partner respects the fact that you have your own life. Just remember that when you've found true love, certain sacrifices may be worth the extra effort. Keep in mind that love conquers all!

17 to 23:

You Maintain Your Balance in the Face of Love

You enjoy being in love, but aren't ready to ignore your other commitments for a date. Your friends and family appreciate the attention you give them, and your partner respects the fact that you have your own life. Sometimes, though, when your partner really needs you, you make the needed adjustment to be there—and your friends understand, since they know you would do the same for them.

24 to 30:
You Would Do Anything for Love

Love and romance are deeply important to you. Your dedication to true love is admirable, but be careful not to shut down the rest of your life while you spend time with your partner. It's crucial that you maintain solid relationships with your family and friends and pursue career and leisure interests. Be careful not to devote yourself to your relationship at the cost of a full, rich life because outside interests and activities can make your relationship stronger. Rather than relying on one relationship to make you happy, value your independence, accomplishments and the friendships you already have.

Are You a Creative Lover?

1. You notice a porno magazine in your lover's apartment. You:

    a. Are repulsed

    b. Are intrigued

    c. Wonder if this means you don't satisfy your lover

    d. Don't really care

2. Your lover asks you to talk dirty in bed. You:

    a. Let loose and have fun with it!

    b. Are not comfortable talking dirty

    c. Say things that would make a porn star blush

    d. Murmur a four-letter word or two, but that's it

3. Your lover wants to role-play in bed. You:

    a. Dig in the closet for a fun outfit

    b. Can't think of anything to say

    c. Respond enthusiastically—you love to improvise

    d. Do it, but feel silly

    e. Would rather not

4. Have you ever made love outdoors?

    a. Never

    b. No, but you would

c. You've thought about it

d. Of course, you love it!

5. S & M is:

a. Disgusting

b. Fun for some people

c. Not for you

d. Awesome!

6. When you have questions about sex, you go to your:

a. Mother

b. Friends

c. Doctor

d. Lover

7. Your lover suggests watching a porno movie instead of foreplay. You:

a. Are against pornography

b. Suggest making your own x-rated video

c. Pull out an x-rated movie from your video collection

d. Agree to try it

8. Your lover wants to try something in the bedroom that you find a little intimidating. You:

a. Go for it enthusiastically

b. Agree after a little prodding

c. Get upset at the suggestion

d. Convince your partner to stick to the ordinary

9. On vacation with your lover, you meet another couple. After a few drinks, they suggest switching partners for the evening. You and your lover:

a. Are flattered but don't consider it

b. Think about it but decide not to

c. Agree to give it a try

d. Feel very uncomfortable, even upset

10. Your ex-partners are likely to describe you as:

a. Great in bed

b. Shy but eager

c. An animal

d. What ex-partners?

11. You have a friend who has been sleeping around. You think your pal is:

a. Promiscuous

b. Liberated

c. Moving too fast and needs to slow down a little

d. Not someone you can relate to anymore

12. The Kama Sutra is:

a. A rock band

b. A Buddhist leader

c. A sexual position

d. The standard work on love in Sanskrit literature

Scoring:

1. a = 1; b = 3; c = 1; d = 2

2. a = 3; b = 1; c = 3; d = 2

3. a = 3; b = 1; c = 3; d = 2; e = 1

4. a = 1; b = 3; c = 2; d = 3

5. a = 1; b = 2; c = 2; d = 3

6. a = 1; b = 2; c = 1; d = 3

7. a = 1; b = 3; c = 3; d = 2

8. a = 3; b = 2; c = 1; d = 1

9. a = 2; b = 2; c = 3; d = 1

10. a = 3; b = 2; c = 3; d = 1

11. a = 1; b = 3; c = 2; d = 1

12. a = 1; b = 1; c = 2; d = 3

● What Your Score Means

12 to 19:

You Need to Relax

When it comes to sex, many things that are delicious, fun and exciting have associated stigmas for you. To really enjoy your body, you need to let go of old phobias or childhood prejudices. If you want to break out of your rut, you need to think about why you are so hesitant to try new things. Even if vanilla is your favorite flavor of ice cream, it won't hurt to try the "flavor of the day" once in a while. And if your lover wants you to do things that you've never done before, why not try it? While you should never put yourself in a risky situation or put yourself in danger in the name of excitement, try to relax . . . a little spice can go a long way!!

20 to 28:

You Are a Creative Lover

You aren't obsessed with excitement but enjoy trying new things. You understand that a healthy sex life needs to include some variety, and are secure enough to allow yourself to delve into the unfamiliar. Even when some practices are beyond your realm, you aren't scared or disgusted by those things that others consider pleasurable. Continue to explore your boundaries, and take pleasure in the knowledge that you have achieved a healthy balance in the bedroom—something that your lover probably takes pleasure in as well!!

29 to 36:

You Have Porn-Star Potential

There are few things you haven't tried, and those you haven't—you just haven't gotten to yet. Nothing is too awkward or unusual for you, and your lovers have been both excited and surprised in the past. Even if you've never heard of it or can't pronounce it, you are more than willing to give it the old college try. Take care that you are not using sexual excitement as a panacea for other issues, and that you aren't putting yourself into possibly risky situations. Exciting is good, but you don't want to get hurt. Have fun . . . and don't forget to buckle your handcuffs!!

Is Your Partner Treating You Well?

1. I believe that my partner thinks about me even when we're not together:

    a. Always

    b. Often

    c. Sometimes

    d. Rarely

    e. Never

2. If I am upset, my partner will notice without my having to mention it:

    a. Always

    b. Often

    c. Sometimes

    d. Rarely

    e. Never

3. My partner makes decisions that affect us both without consulting me:

    a. Always

    b. Often

    c. Sometimes

    d. Rarely

    e. Never

4. When we make plans to do something together, I have to remind my partner about them:

    a. Always

    b. Often

    c. Sometimes

    d. Rarely

    e. Never

5. My partner enjoys making thoughtful gestures:

    a. Always

    b. Often

    c. Sometimes

    d. Rarely

    e. Never

6. My partner makes an effort to share my interests:

    a. Always

    b. Often

    c. Sometimes

    d. Rarely

    e. Never

7. My partner is easily distracted when we're together:

    a. Always

    b. Often

    c. Sometimes

d. Rarely

e. Never

8. My partner really listens to me:

    a. Always

    b. Often

    c. Sometimes

    d. Rarely

    e. Never

9. When I tell my partner that I am upset about something, I believe that he/she will try to avoid doing it in the future:

    a. Always

    b. Often

    c. Sometimes

    d. Rarely

    e. Never

10. My partner lets me know that I am important:

    a. Always

    b. Often

    c. Sometimes

    d. Rarely

    e. Never

11. My partner encourages me to be successful:

    a. Always

b. Often

c. Sometimes

d. Rarely

e. Never

Scoring:

1. a = 5; b = 4; c = 3; d = 2; e = 1	7. a = 1; b = 2; c = 3; d = 4; e = 5
2. a = 5; b = 4; c = 3; d = 2; e = 1	8. a = 5; b = 4; c = 3; d = 2; e = 1
3. a = 1; b = 2; c = 3; d = 4; e = 5	9. a = 5; b = 4; c = 3; d = 2; e = 1
4. a = 1; b = 2; c = 3; d = 4; e = 5	10. a = 5; b = 4; c = 3; d = 2; e = 1
5. a = 5; b = 4; c = 3; d = 2; e = 1	11. a = 5; b = 4; c = 3; d = 2; e = 1
6. a = 5; b = 4; c = 3; d = 2; e = 1	

● What Your Score Means

11 to 25:

Looks Like It's Time for You to Reconsider

You may want to ask yourself what you're getting out of this relationship. All of us need to feel that we are important to our partners. This means more than simply being committed to being together; it means they are committed to knowing who we are and what makes us happy. Your partner is not treating you as a priority, and that spells trouble. Be careful of staying in a relationship that doesn't meet your needs just because the prospect of starting over— or being single—is too intimidating. You deserve to be with someone who makes you a priority and treats you well.

26 to 40:

Your Future Together Looks Bright

You have a partner who cares about you and knows how to show it. S/he may not be perfect, but who is? The trick now is to take the strong foundation that the two of you have established and keep building. You're in luck—very often the hardest thing to do is to talk, and you have a partner who is willing to do just that. Find a way to communicate whatever else you need—and don't forget to listen to what you hear in return.

41 to 55:

You've Struck It Rich

No doubt about it, you have a partner who has mastered the art of consideration. But this isn't something that your partner could do without your involvement—respect and commitment of this variety is a two-way street. Both of you understand what it means to form a relationship, to work together to create a bond that holds long after the infatuation of the first few months has begun to fade. Congratulations, a romance this caring is hard to find.

Is Your Partner Too Controlling?

1. Usually, the plans for the weekend are:

   a. Dictated by your partner

   b. Dictated by you

   c. A compromise

   d. Worked out together as you go along

2. When you're out together at a restaurant:

   a. You partner likes to order for both of you

   b. You both order independently

   c. You decide what to order together

   d. Your partner asks you to decide for both of you

3. Generally, arguments end when:

   a. You resolve the issue together

   b. You give up and your partner "wins"

   c. Your partner storms out of the room

   d. You both lose your voices, a result of the screaming match

4. How often does your partner tell you what to wear?

   a. Rarely

   b. Only when I ask for my partner's opinion

   c. Every day

   d. Frequently

5. When you want to go out on your own with your friends, your partner:

    a. Says "have fun"

    b. Tells you that you can go, but you must be back by a certain time

    c. Doesn't want you going out unless you're together

    d. Makes separate plans

6. When it comes to money and your relationship, your partner:

    a. Wants to know how you spend all your money

    b. Wants to approve of how you spend your money

    c. Doesn't keep tabs on your spending habits

    d. Thinks you should discuss big purchases before making them

7. How often do you find yourself changing your behavior to meet your partner's expectations and/or to avoid negative consequences (i.e., punishment) from your partner?

    a. Always

    b. Often

    c. Sometimes

    d. Occasionally

    e. Never

8. You're home with your partner when the phone rings. Your partner:

    a. Always answers the phone

    b. Always wants you to answer the phone

   c. Makes you ignore the phone and lets it ring until the machine picks up

   d. Will answer the phone if it's nearby

9. If you and your partner gathered a group for dinner, who would put together the guest list?

   a. You would choose the people to invite

   b. Your partner would choose the people to invite

   c. You would both decide on a fun group

   d. You would each invite half of the group

10. When you ask your partner for an opinion on an offer for a new job, your partner:

   a. Tells you whether or not to take it

   b. Helps you determine the move that's best for you

   c. Listens but will not make a choice either way

   d. Acknowledges that it's your decision, but tells you what s/he thinks you should do

Scoring:

1. a = 1; b = 3; c = 2; d = 2	**6.** a = 2; b = 1; c = 3; d = 2
2. a = 1; b = 2; c = 2; d = 3	**7.** a = 1; b = 1; c = 2; d = 3; e = 3
3. a = 3; b = 1; c = 1; d = 2	**8.** a = 1; b = 3; c = 1; d = 2
4. a = 2; b = 3; c = 1; d = 1	**9.** a = 3; b = 1; c = 2; d = 2
5. a = 3; b = 1; c = 1; d = 2	**10.** a = 1; b = 3; c = 3; d = 2

● What Your Score Means

10 to 16:
Control Corner

Some people have controlling interests in companies; your partner has a controlling interest in you. It appears as if your every action, thought and feeling must be approved, monitored and defined by your partner. This is not healthy for either of you. As difficult as it may be, you need to set about repairing this relationship if you want to save it, or jump ship altogether. Sometimes the only thing you can do is get out of this type of relationship and get counseling so you don't repeat the same patterns. You deserve a relationship that supports you and gives you the independence to control your own life.

17 to 23:
Limited Control

Although you have some autonomy, your partner can be controlling and may try to ordain the course of the relationship. Sometimes people manifest controlling behaviors out of fear—fear that they'll be abandoned, fear that if anything is out of control, everything will get out of control, etc. If it's possible, approach your partner about this need for control. Provide concrete examples and try to understand the motivation behind the attempts to dominate. If you can't make any headway toward a relationship where you both are in equal control, make an exit.

24 to 30:
Control Free

For the most part, you and your sweetheart are indeed partners in your relationship. Occasionally it may seem that your partner is in control, but it may be in just one particular situation. Rather than having one person be in control of the other person or the relationship itself, you two generally act as co-pilots. You take each other's opinions and needs into account and chart the course together. Your relationship with your partner is all about reciprocal give and take; one partner does not dominate the other. This type of relationship is based on equality and mutual respect. You and your partner communicate with each other very well and strive to fulfill each other's wishes. Sometimes you have to make compromises, but that's what relationships are all about.

Do You Try to Control Your Partner?

1. With whom do you and your partner spend holidays?

   a. With your family/friends

   b. Alone with each other

   c. With your partner's family/friends

   d. You alternate holidays with your partner's family/friends and your own

2. You're shopping with your partner when you catch someone flirting with your honey. You:

   a. Say something to scare the flirt away

   b. Get mad at your partner

   c. Laugh about the situation with your partner

   d. Put your arm around your partner so the flirt knows to get lost

3. What is your reaction when your partner doesn't do what you would want?

   a. You pout for a few minutes and then move on

   b. You are rude until you get your way

   c. You accept it and move on

   d. You yell

4. If you did not like your partner's friends, you would:

   a. Make your partner choose between them and you

   b. Not allow your partner to hang out with them

   c. Respect them simply because they're your partner's friends

   d. Choose not to hang out with them, but don't mind that your partner does

5. How do you feel about your partner being friends with an ex?

   a. You don't mind if s/he's your friend, too

   b. Doesn't matter to you

   c. You don't like it but you tolerate it

   d. You would not permit it

6. When you're in your partner's apartment and the telephone rings, you:

   a. Let your partner answer it

   b. Attempt to answer the phone because you want to know who's calling

   c. Bug your partner to tell you who is on the phone after the first hello

   d. Answer the phone if it's closest to you

7. If you didn't like your partner's outfit, you would:

   a. Joke about it

   b. Politely give your opinion

   c. Say nothing

   d. Make your partner change clothes

8. Your significant other decides that it's time for a major career change. You would expect your partner to:

    a. Figure it out alone and let you know about any new plans

    b. Get your permission before making any changes

    c. Talk to you once it's time to make a big decision

    d. Get your advice from the beginning

9. When you and your honey go on a date, who usually decides what you'll do?

    a. The two of you alternate

    b. Your partner does

    c. You do

    d. Both of you decide together

10. If your honey were to upset you in front of a group of friends, your reaction would be to:

    a. Discuss it when the two of you were alone

    b. Discuss it in front of them

    c. Make a scene

    d. Forget about it altogether

Scoring:

1. a = 3; b = 1; c = 1; d = 2	6. a = 1; b = 3; c = 3; d = 2
2. a = 3; b = 3; c = 1; d = 2	7. a = 2; b = 2; c = 1; d = 3
3. a = 2; b = 3; c = 1; d = 3	8. a = 1; b = 3; c = 2; d = 2
4. a = 3; b = 3; c = 2; d = 1	9. a = 2; b = 1; c = 3; d = 2
5. a = 1; b = 1; c = 2; d = 3	10. a = 1; b = 2; c = 3; d = 1

• What Your Score Means

10 to 16:

You Stay out of Your Partner's Business

You do a great job staying out of your partner's business and trying not to control things. Perhaps you are aware that people get scared off when others try to control them, which may make you afraid of overstepping boundaries. However, if you want to have a serious relationship, it won't hurt for you to be involved in your partner's life. It's okay to give your opinion, advice and support, when needed. If you do this in a supportive manner, it will be appreciated. Give it a try—you might be surprised at how much stronger this makes your relationship.

17 to 23:

You Are a Balanced Partner

You let your honey have freedom without too much interference from you. You may slightly overstep the boundaries every once in awhile, and be a little too involved in your partner's decisions, however, you probably do this because you want what's best for them and you want to show that you care. If you're able to catch yourself when you start to overstep boundaries, then your relationship has potential to be fulfilling for both of you.

24 to 30:

You Might Be a Control Freak

You seem to be trying to control most aspects of your partner's life. You make so many decisions for both of you that your partner practically needs to ask your permission before doing anything independently. Is this the kind of relationship that is satisfying for either of you? Perhaps you feel that you have so little control over other aspects of your life that you need to tell your significant other what to do. Or maybe you just don't trust enough to let your partner "roam free" every once in awhile. Whatever the reason, you feel that you must have the power in your relationship. How long do you really think your honey will put up with this? And how long do you want to? You will both get a lot more out of a relationship built on mutual trust and respect. Give it a try!

Is It Time to Meet Your Partner's Family?

1. How long have you and your partner been together?

   a. A few weeks

   b. Less than a few months, but it has been very intense

   c. Six months to a year

   d. More than a year

2. Where do you envision your relationship in a year?

   a. Not sure

   b. Hopefully we'll be together

   c. I imagine it'll be even more serious

   d. I haven't thought that far ahead

3. Has your partner ever met *your* family?

   a. Yes, on a few occasions

   b. No, but they are geographically quite far away

   c. No, but we are making arrangements for it to happen

   d. Never

4. Are you comfortable discussing your employment and career prospects with new people?

   a. Sure—I'm a great storyteller and can even make my job sound interesting!

b. Sure—I love any opportunity to talk about myself

c. I guess—as long as no one asks how much I'm making

d. Not really

5. Are there any significant religious or cultural differences between you and your partner?

a. Yes, and we have discussed them with our families

b. Not really—we come from similar backgrounds

c. A few, but I don't consider them insurmountable

d. Yes, and I feel awkward discussing them with my partner

6. What would you like to discover about your partner by meeting his/her family?

a. I'd like to be prepared for whether my partner will age well

b. I'd love to hear cute stories about my honey as a child

c. I've often wondered what kind of wonderful people produced such a wonderful person

d. I'm hoping to figure out whether the qualities that annoy me will get worse as my partner gets older

7. How much do you feel that you already know about the family of your honey?

a. I've heard a few stories, but I don't know too much

b. Just basic facts like names and ages of siblings

c. With how much my partner talks about them, I could probably write a family history

d. My partner and I never discuss our families

8. Have you heard any horror stories about the way that your partner's family has treated past significant others?

   a. My partner hasn't been serious enough with anyone else to bring them home

   b. No—but I hadn't thought to ask!

   c. No—my partner's family sounds far too sweet to ever do such a thing

   d. Yes, but I think that I could avoid that person's mistakes

   e. Yes, and I'm frightened

9. Do you and your partner ever discuss having a family of your own?

   a. Yes, often

   b. Occasionally

   c. Never

   d. My current partner is not someone I'd consider having a family with

10. What are your expectations about meeting your partner's kin?

   a. I imagine that it will bring us to a new level of intimacy

   b. I hope that it'll give me a firmer grip on my partner's affections

   c. I think that how I get along with the family will make or break us as a couple

   d. I hope that I'll get to see a new side of the person whom I love

   e. I'm not sure what to expect, but I imagine that it will be fun

Scoring:

1. a = 1; b = 2; c = 3; d = 3

2. a = 1; b = 2; c = 3; d = 1

3. a = 3; b = 2; c = 2; d = 1

4. a = 3; b = 3; c = 2; d = 1

5. a = 3; b = 3; c = 2; d = 1

6. a = 2; b = 3; c = 3; d = 1

7. a = 2; b = 2; c = 3; d = 3

8. a = 3; b = 2; c = 3; d = 2; e = 1

9. a = 3; b = 2; c = 1; d = 1

10. a = 3; b = 1; c = 1; d = 3; e = 2

• What Your Score Means

10 to 16:
Fools Rush in (to Other People's Families)

Imagine yourself sitting at the kitchen table where your partner's family eats dinner every night, having said something so awkward and inappropriate that you wish that you had never opened your mouth. This, unfortunately, could be you—if you rush in to meet your honey's family before the two of you are ready to take such a significant step. It could be that you and your sweetie just aren't serious enough yet to make that kind of a leap; it also could be that you're insecure about your own social skills and aren't sure that you'll make a good impression. In any case, you should definitely do some evaluation—about yourself, your relationship and your motives about wanting to meet your partner's family—before you go offering to bring the mashed potatoes for Thanksgiving. Back off, baby! All in good time!

17 to 23:
Almost a Family Affair

While meeting your partner's relatives at this point in your relationship probably wouldn't be *destructive* to your love affair, it's not necessarily the best time to make this step. Maybe you and your partner aren't yet secure enough in your feelings for one another to expose your relationship to the scrutiny of relatives' prying eyes; maybe you simply haven't discussed the ramifications of such a significant meeting. In any case, better to take a little time to learn more about each other, and strengthen your relationship, before you move to this stage. Look before you leap!

24 to 30:
Meet the Parents

Get ready to gush over baby pictures and laugh at family stories . . . it looks like you're ready to meet your partner's family! You and your partner have a solid, intimate relationship with a shared set of values; getting to know each other's closest kin is a logical next stage in advancing to a new level of togetherness. Just be sure to relax and be yourself; surely, the qualities that your partner loves about you will be immediately apparent to the people your partner grew up with. Good luck!

Keeping the Flame Alive

Are the two of you treating each other like lovers, or like two people stuck on a ship called "relationship"? These self-evaluations are best shared with a partner. Often the issues raised here are important to one or both of you, but as is the case with many relationship problems, these issues are never expressed. Or if they are brought to light, it's in anger, after the damage has been done. With proper communication, to yourself and to each other, the flame can burn forever.

Is There Passion in Your Relationship?

1. When you kiss your partner, you feel:

   a. Tingly

   b. Cozy

   c. Hot

   d. Nothing

2. On average, how many times a day do you and your partner express affection for each other?

   a. None

   b. One

   c. Two

   d. Three or more

3. How often do you and your partner try new things in bed?

   a. Never

   b. Rarely

   c. Sometimes

   d. Often

   e. All the time

4. The lines of communication between you and your partner are:

   a. Crossed—we need to get them to go in the same direction

b. Open and clear

c. Cut—we need to reestablish them

d. Sometimes obstructed by a busy signal, but we're working on them

5. How much uninterrupted time do you and your partner generally spend together?

a. An hour a day

b. A couple of hours a week

c. A few hours a month

d. Not much—we're constantly interrupted by work and other commitments

6. You and your partner try out new romantic activities together:

a. Often so that we can maintain some freshness in our relationship

b. Never because we're set in a routine

c. Every now and then when we feel we're in a rut and completely bored in our relationship

d. Only when my partner takes the initiative

7. How often do you find that you can't control your passion and must spontaneously seek out your partner for romance, even when you're supposed to be doing something else (e.g., work)?

a. Never

b. Rarely

c. Sometimes

d. Often

e. All the time

8. How often do you surprise your partner with something special—a gift, a great date, a meal, etc.?

a. Never

b. Rarely

c. Sometimes

d. Often

e. All the time

9. How often does your partner surprise you with something special—a gift, a great date, a meal, etc.?

a. Never

b. Rarely

c. Sometimes

d. Often

e. All the time

10. Everyone likes to feel appreciated, especially in a relationship. You:

a. Tend to take your partner and the relationship for granted

b. Look forward to your time together and try not to waste a moment

c. Recognize the value of your relationship and do your best to treat your partner well

d. Go through stages; sometimes you're great at showing your appreciation and other times you forget to make the effort

Scoring:

1. a = 3; b = 2; c = 3; d = 1	6. a = 3; b = 1; c = 2; d = 2
2. a = 1; b = 2; c = 2; d = 3	7. a = 1; b = 1; c = 2; d = 3; e = 3
3. a = 1; b = 1; c = 2; d = 3; e = 3	8. a = 1; b = 1; c = 2; d = 3; e = 3
4. a = 1; b = 3; c = 1; d = 2	9. a = 1; b = 1; c = 2; d = 3; e = 3
5. a = 3; b = 2; c = 1; d = 1	10. a = 1; b = 3; c = 3; d = 2

• What Your Score Means

10 to 16:
Where's the Passion?

Instead of fanning the flames of desire, it seems like you're always trying to stifle the yawn that is your relationship. Are you and your partner just currently experiencing some downtime in your relationship, or has it always been like this? If you're satisfied, that's one thing, but if you want to add some passion to your love life, try some new activities. For example, maybe you could plan for a secret rendezvous so you can look forward to getting away together. Try sending each other racy letters or voicemail or email messages to keep the spark alive when you're not together.

17 to 23:
Passion Potential

There are some sparks, but it wouldn't hurt to go foraging for some kindling. To promote passion, you need to learn to be better partners to each other. Improving your communication with your partner will intensify your relationship, because you'll be better able to fulfill each other's needs. Try to spend more time in physical contact with each other, even if you're just holding hands. When you ignite your relationship, you'll want to spend as much time as possible together.

24 to 30:
Pure Passion

You've hit the passion-prize jackpot! You and your partner seem committed to developing an exciting relationship, one that is unlikely to fizzle out. To maintain this level of vigor, you and your partner should continue to try new things and keep the communication lines open. By consciously striving to keep things exciting, dynamic and passionate, you're working to ensure a long-lasting and satisfying relationship.

How Spicy Is Your Relationship?

1. You are sexually intimate with your partner:

   a. Every day

   b. 2–3 times a week

   c. 4–5 times a week

   d. Hardly ever

2. When you dress for bed, you typically wear:

   a. Nothing at all

   b. Flannel or cotton pajamas

   c. Anything that's sexy

   d. Something that you know your lover finds cute

3. Your sex life would be described as:

   a. Interesting

   b. Adventurous

   c. Routine

   d. Emotional

4. When you fight with your partner, you:

   a. Scream and yell

   b. Give each other the cold shoulder

c. Wind up having sex in the middle

d. Debate until you reach a compromise

e. You never fight

5. Your relationship is full of:

a. Surprises

b. Predictability

c. Comfort

d. Spontaneity

6. You fight with your partner:

a. Often

b. Never

c. Occasionally

d. More often than not

7. Having sex with your partner typically involves:

a. One favorite position

b. Multiple positions that you couldn't name

c. A couple of positions

d. Multiple positions and locations

8. When you go out in public, you and your partner:

a. Introduce each other as friends

b. Hold hands or put your arm around each other

c. Can't keep your hands off each other

d. Show affection when appropriate

9. Your partner pulls out a sex toy during foreplay. You:

a. Scream with delight

b. Scream in horror

c. Decide to try it despite initial reservations

d. Think it is disgusting and feel rejected that he/she wants a mechanical device to satisfy him/her

e. Choose not to try it but use it for inspiration to revive your sex life

10. A fun night out with your partner is:

a. A distant memory of the past

b. A frequent occurrence

c. An occasional treat

d. A sure thing when you have time for it

Scoring:

1. a = 3; b = 2; c = 3; d = 1	**6.** a = 3; b = 1; c = 2; d = 3
2. a = 3; b = 1; c = 3; d = 2	**7.** a = 1; b = 3; c = 2; d = 3
3. a = 2; b = 3; c = 1; d = 2	**8.** a = 1; b = 2; c = 3; d = 2
4. a = 3; b = 1; c = 3; d = 2; e = 1	**9.** a = 3; b = 1; c = 2; d = 1; e = 2
5. a = 3; b = 1; c = 2; d = 3	**10.** a = 1; b = 3; c = 1; d = 2

• What Your Score Means

10 to 16:
Your Relationship Needs Some Pepper

Has your relationship settled into complacency? If you feel that things are a little too comfortable, you may need to add a dash of romance or the occasional element of surprise to spice things up! Everyone needs to feel desired—so consider surprising your partner with some sexy underwear or a romantic love letter. Relationships take effort and thought to keep things fresh and exciting over time.

17 to 23:
Your Relationship Is Moderately Spicy

You balance spice with sugar in your relationship for the perfect blend of spiciness. You keep romance alive and interest in each other peaked without resorting to fights for attention. Consideration for your partner and friendship add romantic flavor in your relationship. Things are comfortable without being boring. You don't need stunts and drama to make things flavorful, your natural patterns are spicy enough!

24 to 30:
Your Relationship Is Hot 'n' Spicy

You sizzle away in your tempestuous, spicy relationship. You like adventure, romance, experimentation and those hot fights, too. Just be careful that the drama in your relationship is for fun and not added as an attempt to get extra attention and create unneeded excitement. A relationship that lasts over time requires friendship and compassion more than spice and sizzle.

Do You Spend Enough Time with Your Partner?

1. You see your partner:

   a. Every day

   b. 4–5 times a week

   c. 2–3 times a week

   d. Once a week

   e. Less than once a week

2. You talk on the phone with your partner:

   a. Multiple times a day

   b. Once a day

   c. Once every couple of days

   d. Once a week or less

3. You go on a date out alone with your partner:

   a. Once a week

   b. Once a month

   c. Can't remember the last time

   d. On a regular basis

4. In your relationship you feel that you are:

   a. Taken for granted

b. Special and appreciated

c. Romanced off your feet

d. Comfortable in a routine

5. You are sexually intimate with your partner:

a. Every day

b. 4–6 times a week

c. 3–4 times a week

d. Once or twice a week

e. A couple of times a month, in a good month

6. On special occasions such as anniversaries, you:

a. Always make it a point to celebrate together

b. Sometimes forget

c. Exchange thoughtful gifts

d. Mention the day, but often don't do anything else extra

7. When you go on vacation, you usually:

a. Go with your partner

b. Go with your family

c. Go with your friends

d. Go with your partner and your family

8. Your friends say that since you've been in a relationship, you:

a. Have disappeared from their lives

b. Still spend all your time with them

c. Are never seen without your partner

d. Make time for everyone in your life

9. You typically have interests and/or hobbies that your partner does not share.

a. True, and you spend most of your time doing things separately

b. False, but you are developing some now

c. True, and you are teaching your partner to share in them now

d. False, you don't have any of your own separate interests

10. If a business trip got cancelled at the last minute, the first person you would call to make plans would be:

a. Definitely your partner

b. Definitely your friends

c. You would call your partner and your friends and try to see everyone in the week ahead

d. You'd make plans with friends because you know you'll see your partner before, after or during plans with other friends

Scoring:

1. a = 3; b = 3; c = 2; d = 1; e = 2	**6.** a = 3; b = 1; c = 3; d = 2
2. a = 3; b = 3; c = 2; d = 1	**7.** a = 3; b = 1; c = 2; d = 3
3. a = 3; b = 2; c = 1; d = 3	**8.** a = 3; b = 1; c = 3; d = 2
4. a = 1; b = 3; c = 3; d = 2	**9.** a = 1; b = 2; c = 2; d = 3
5. a = 3; b = 3; c = 2; d = 2; e = 1	**10.** a = 3; b = 1; c = 2; d = 3

● What Your Score Means

10 to 16:
Not a Lot of Time for the Relationship

If you can't, don't or won't make time for your partner, then the romance is sure to fizzle instead of sizzle. If you love the person whom you are with, make sure that they have the appropriate place in your list of priorities. How you spend your time indicates what is important to you, and if you don't want to spend time with your partner, you are sending a loud message about your feelings. If your partner is the obstacle to your seeing one another, then you should consider discussing this and determining if you're satisfied with what your partner has to give.

17 to 23:
Seeking Balance in Life

Just because you are in a relationship, you don't have to lose yourself in the process or lose your friends. You make time for your relationship, family, friends and most important, yourself. This way your partner enhances your life instead of taking it over. Just make sure that your honey knows how you feel and that extra thought is put into keeping the romance alive.

24 to 30:
Attached at the Hip

Since you've been in this relationship, your friends are probably wondering where you've disappeared to. You spend plenty of time with your partner, but ask yourself if it is too much time. Sometimes we can become dependent in relationships and lose our sense of self in the process. Try to devote a little of yourself to other endeavors and people in your life. You shouldn't have to sacrifice your relationship in the process, it should only become stronger as you both find balance in your lives.

Does Your World Revolve around Your Partner?

1. Your best friend asks you to a hot new club on Saturday, but you usually spend Saturday nights with your partner. You:

    a. Go with your friend. After all, you don't actually have *plans* with your partner

    b. Turn down your friend so you can keep Saturday night for your honey

    c. Get a group together to go to the club, including your friend and your partner

    d. See if your partner would mind spending time together during the day instead

2. You just got a dream job, but it's in another state. You:

    a. Accept the offer without a second thought

    b. Decline. You could never be that far away from your partner

    c. Ask your partner to move with you, or discuss a long-distance relationship

    d. Agonize over the decision until the deadline passes

3. Two weeks before you and your partner are to leave for a vacation to Europe, your partner's boss says there's no way s/he can take the time off. You:

    a. Forget the vacation; you can't go without your partner

b. Go yourself and have the time of your life

c. See if a friend wants to take his/her place

d. Reschedule for a time when both of you can go

4. You get a last-minute work assignment just before leaving for a romantic evening with your partner that you both planned weeks ago. You:

a. Tell your boss that you can't do it because you have unbreakable plans

b. Tell your boss you'll have to come in early in the morning to finish the assignment

c. Cancel your date

d. Have dinner with your partner, but cut the date short to go back to the office

5. You're about to leave for a day at the beach with your friends when your partner calls to complain about a horrible cold. You:

a. Suggest some Tylenol and call your partner from the beach to check in

b. Make some chicken soup for your partner before going to the beach with your pals

c. Cancel your plans and take care of your honey

d. Come home early from the beach to keep your honey company

6. You told your partner that you'd call at five P.M., but you're stuck in a meeting. You:

a. Call right after the meeting

b. Excuse yourself from the meeting to make the call on time

    c. Call after the meeting and then stop by on your way home to apologize by cooking dinner

    d. Call after the meeting whenever you get a chance

7. You're going to the movies with a friend who wants to see a movie that your partner really wants to see. You:

    a. Tell your friend you two will have to see something else

    b. See the movie. It's dumb to "reserve" movies for your partner

    c. See the movie with your friend and then see it again with your partner

    d. See the movie with your friend and don't tell your partner about it

8. Your partner tells you about expensive sunglasses that s/he really wants, but can't afford. You:

    a. Help your partner figure out a budget so s/he can save for them

    b. Buy them as a gift, though you really can't afford them either

    c. Promise to get them as a birthday present in a few months

    d. Encourage your partner to find a cheaper pair

9. You two get in bed but you're really not in the mood. Your partner is clearly in the mood. You:

    a. Say you have a headache

    b. Give in. You aim to please

    c. Say good night, roll over and go to sleep

    d. Suggest cuddling instead

10. Your partner was supposed to call you at noon. It's three P.M. and no call. You:

a. Call your partner

b. Go out looking for your partner to see why there's been no call

c. Do nothing. You're pissed and you'll make that clear when you speak eventually

d. Do nothing—it was only a phone call

Scoring:

1. a = 1; b = 3; c = 2; d = 2

2. a = 1; b = 3; c = 2; d = 3

3. a = 3; b = 1; c = 1; d = 2

4. a = 3; b = 3; c = 1; d = 2

5. a = 1; b = 2; c = 3; d = 2

6. a = 2; b = 3; c = 3; d = 1

7. a = 3; b = 1; c = 2; d = 2

8. a = 2; b = 3; c = 2; d = 1

9. a = 2; b = 3; c = 1; d = 2

10. a = 2; b = 3; c = 1; d = 1

• What Your Score Means

10 to 16:

Your World Revolves around *You*:

You know what it takes to make you happy and that's what you'll do, no matter what. If you continue along this path, you may lose your relationship. Of course, you should take care of yourself, but remember that if you really care for your partner, you need to think about how your actions and choices will affect this person as well as you. A healthy relationship involves give and take; you clearly understand the take part but you may want to put some more effort into the give.

17 to 23:

Your World Revolves around Both of You

You do a great job taking you and your relationship into account when making decisions. You are neither selfish nor selfless. Not all of your choices need to involve your partner, which means that when you do consider your significant other, it's because you want to and because you care. You clearly understand that you can't love someone else without loving and caring for yourself first.

24 to 30:

Your World Revolves around Your Partner

You often make decisions based on what's good for your partner, rather than what's good for you. While it is laudable to care about someone else's needs, you must remember that your needs matter as well. If you allow yourself to become overly focused on your partner, you may wind up in a smothering, unbalanced relationship. You may also end up unhappy because no one is taking care of you. Make sure that there is give and take, not just give. Take a good look at yourself and figure out what you need to do to make you happy—and then make sure you ask for it.

Who Has the Power in Your Relationship?

1. Who earns more money?

   a. You

   b. Your partner

   c. You both earn roughly the same amount

   d. You aren't sure

2. When you go out at night:

   a. You usually decide on the plans

   b. Your partner usually makes the plans

   c. You both choose where to go together

   d. You alternate on who makes the plans

3. On holidays, you:

   a. Celebrate most of them with your family

   b. Celebrate most of them with your partner's family

   c. Try to split up the celebrations 50/50 between the two families

   d. Celebrate with both families together for holiday parties

4. You generally hang out with:

   a. Your friends

   b. Your partner's friends

c. Each other alone

d. Both sets of friends equally

5. On the topic of commitment:

a. You want more

b. Your partner wants more

c. You are both happy with the present situation

d. Neither of you is ready for greater commitment

e. You never discuss commitment

6. If you were in a long-distance relationship, who would travel more frequently to see the other person?

a. You would

b. Your partner would

c. You would take turns

d. Whoever can afford to travel more in terms of time and money would make the trip

7. If you broke up with your partner today:

a. You would have an easier time adjusting

b. Your partner would have an easier time adjusting

c. You both would rebound at about the same pace

d. You'd both be stuck in a rut

8. If one person in the relationship got an important career opportunity in another city:

a. You would both move to be near the other person

b. You would move, but your partner would not

c. Your partner would move, but you would not

d. Neither one would move to be near the other

9. You consider yourself:

a. More physically attractive than your partner

b. Less physically attractive than your partner

c. Roughly the same physical attractiveness

d. You don't know who is more physically attractive

10. Your partner gets concert tickets to a favorite group on the night of your friend's birthday party. You:

a. Go to the party alone while your partner goes to the concert

b. Go to the party together and forget the concert

c. Go to the party together and leave early to catch the second half of the concert

d. Both miss the party and go to the concert together

Scoring:

1. a = 1; b = 3; c = 2; d = 2	**6.** a = 3; b = 1; c = 2; d = 2
2. a = 1; b = 3; c = 2; d = 2	**7.** a = 1; b = 3; c = 2; d = 2
3. a = 1; b = 3; c = 2; d = 2	**8.** a = 2; b = 3; c = 1; d = 2
4. a = 1; b = 3; c = 2; d = 2	**9.** a = 1; b = 3; c = 2; d = 2
5. a = 3; b = 1; c = 2; d = 2; e = 2	**10.** a = 3; b = 1; c = 2; d = 3

• What Your Score Means

10 to 16:

You've Got the Power

You control this relationship, and you probably know it. You make the important decisions and basically call the shots from the finances to your social calendar. Is this pattern typical in your relationships (romantic and otherwise)? Do you choose friends and romantic partners who allow you to run the show or do you prefer companions who contribute on a more equal basis? If you prefer submissiveness to a challenge, consider what needs these partners fill for you. While you may think you need to be in control, you may be happier if you find a way to share some of the responsibility and experience a more even relationship.

17 to 23:

Even Power Distribution

You have achieved a balance of power in your relationship. From time to time, the control may sway and shift and put one person in a greater position of control. But this is only natural, and in your case, evens out over time. The important thing is that this relationship is based on give and take. You support and encourage each other; you care for your partner and feel comfortable being cared for in return.

24 to 30:

Your Partner Has the Power

Your partner is the one who has more power in your relationship. Are you satisfied with this arrangement? You may enjoy feeling that someone is taking care of you and handling the big decisions. The danger, however, is that you may be in a relationship where your partner doesn't value you as an equal. Take a close look at your relationship and figure out if you are being treated with the respect and equality that you deserve. Sharing the decisions and consequent responsibility may make you both happier in the end.

How Considerate Are You Toward Your Significant Other?

1. The book that your partner wants to bring on vacation is only in stock at a bookstore across town. There's no way your honey can take time from work to get there before the trip. While it's not convenient for you, you could slip out of work and get it. You:

    a. Tell your partner to forget the book

    b. Get the book for your partner

    c. Help your partner find another book in a store that's convenient for both of you

    d. Get a similar book for your partner in a shop nearby

2. After a busy week, you're looking forward to a quiet night at home. Your partner wants to go out to a party. You:

    a. Go to the party to make your partner happy

    b. Stay in

    c. Agree to go to the party for a little while

    d. Compromise and go out but do something mellow like a movie instead

3. Your partner has been talking about problems at work so much lately that even though you always want to help and listen, it's making you crazy. You:

    a. Suggest going for a run. It will reduce your partner's stress and you can't talk while running

b. Listen to the work stories again

c. Respond to every example with an equally irritating thing about your own office situation

d. Get a pencil and paper and start making a list of ways to deal with the problem

4. You're at a restaurant and your partner does not like the entrée that s/he ordered but loves your meal. When your honey asks you to split both dinners, you:

a. Say no because you like yours much better

b. Share both dishes

c. Split your meal and order another dish to share

d. Give another taste of your entrée but refuse to share the whole meal

5. You are traveling on business and want to save money by staying with your ex, in whom you have no interest. Your partner is uncomfortable with the idea. You:

a. Say you'll stay at a hotel but really stay with your ex

b. Stay at a hotel

c. Agree to stay in a hotel if your partner splits the bill

d. Stay with your ex only after assuring your partner at length that you have no interest in your former flame

6. A little while into a day of hiking, your partner complains of blisters and wants to turn back. Disappointed at the idea of missing the hike, you:

a. Decide to go on alone

b. Bandage the blisters and encourage your partner to try a little more

c. Agree to turn back but give your partner a hard time about it for the rest of the day

d. Head home and plan a great alternate activity

7. After you make a rude comment to your partner, you realize you've been taking your stress out on the person you love. You:

a. Apologize for your behavior

b. Keep quiet and tell yourself you shouldn't have been provoked

c. Keep quiet but make a mental note to try to be nice in the future

d. Make a joke about it and make an effort to be nice

8. Your partner runs into an ex who is with a new partner. It is the first time they've seen each other since the breakup, and your partner seems upset by the encounter. You:

a. Mention the problematic issues in the old relationship so your partner will be reminded of why they broke up

b. Tell your partner you don't feel comfortable talking about an ex

c. Are extra loving so that s/he remembers that s/he has found a much greener pasture

d. Make it clear that you're there to listen if s/he wants to talk about it

9. Your partner calls you at work several times a day. You find it distracting and think your coworkers may be starting to notice. You:

a. Screen your calls and don't answer if it's your partner

b. Answer the calls but continue to work while you're on the phone

c. Ask your partner not to call you at work but offer to call once a day when it's a quiet time for you at the office

d. Explain the situation and agree to talk every day at lunchtime

10. You don't like your partner's best friend and they have a fight. You:

a. Mention that they have a long history together and that it's not worth holding a grudge

b. Encourage your partner to end the friendship

c. Be supportive without offering an opinion

d. Say that you'd prefer to stay out of it

Scoring:

1. a = 1; b = 3; c = 2; d = 2	**6.** a = 1; b = 2; c = 2; d = 3
2. a = 3; b = 1; c = 2; d = 2	**7.** a = 3; b = 1; c = 2; d = 3
3. a = 2; b = 3; c = 1; d = 3	**8.** a = 2; b = 1; c = 3; d = 3
4. a = 1; b = 3; c = 3; d = 2	**9.** a = 1; b = 1; c = 2; d = 3
5. a = 1; b = 3; c = 2; d = 2	**10.** a = 3; b = 1; c = 2; d = 2

● What Your Score Means

10 to 16:

Your Attitude Is Me First!

You're doing a great job taking care of yourself. However, you may not be doing a good enough job taking care of your partner.

How Well Do You Really Know Your Partner?

1. When it comes to your partner's exes, you know:

    a. Everything

    b. A fair amount

    c. A little

    d. Nothing

2. Do you know the middle names and birthdays of all the members of your partner's immediate family?

    a. No

    b. Some of them

    c. Yes

    d. Most of them

3. Your partner is given a choice of three meals. You'd know the choice:

    a. Only if you made a lucky guess

    b. Probably

    c. Maybe

    d. Definitely

4. Your partner's religious/spiritual beliefs are:

    a. A total mystery to you

b. Fairly known to you

c. Entirely familiar to you

d. Kind of hazy to you

5. How well do you know your partner's greatest fear?

a. With certainty

b. You're pretty sure

c. Not at all

d. You're not even sure if your partner has a greatest fear

6. Your knowledge of how your partner voted in the last presidential election is:

a. Total

b. Pretty certain

c. Pretty uncertain

d. You don't know at all

7. Your partner thinks that astrology is:

a. You have no idea

b. Ridiculous

c. You're not sure, but you can guess

d. Wonderful

8. When it comes to your partner's medical history, you:

a. Know every last detail

b. Have a decent sense of it

c. Know how much your partner hates going to see a doctor

d. Cannot provide any information

9. How sure are you about what your partner does all day at work?

a. You barely understand your partner's job

b. You know it more or less

c. You know about the big projects but not the little details

d. You have a detailed idea of how your partner spends the day

10. You finish your partner's sentences:

a. Never

b. Rarely

c. Sometimes

d. Often

e. All the time

Scoring:

1. a = 1; b = 2; c = 2; d = 3	6. a = 1; b = 2; c = 2; d = 3
2. a = 3; b = 2; c = 1; d = 1	7. a = 3; b = 1; c = 2; d = 1
3. a = 3; b = 2; c = 2; d = 1	8. a = 1; b = 1; c = 2; d = 3
4. a = 3; b = 1; c = 1; d = 2	9. a = 3; b = 2; c = 2; d = 1
5. a = 1; b = 2; c = 3; d = 3	10. a = 3; b = 3; c = 2; d = 1; e = 1

● What Your Score Means

10 to 16:
You Know Your Partner Inside and Out

You know your partner extraordinarily well. From food preferences to political beliefs, you've paid total attention to what your partner likes, dislikes, believes and disdains. Gushing with information about your honey, you might even know this person better than you know yourself!

17 to 23:
A Touch of Mystery

You've spent time with your partner, and along the way you've learned a thing or two. So maybe you can't predict every move that this person will make or every word that will be said, but who would want to? You know that you like who your honey is, and no detail about this person's past, present or future can top that nugget of knowledge. Besides, a little intrigue adds spice to the relationship.

24 to 30:
What's Your Name Again?

Whether you've been together ten weeks or ten years, you've sure got a lot to learn about your partner. One can certainly have too much information, but one can also have too little. Since your side of the relationship seems to be all about mysteries and puzzles, you might consider initiating a game of fill-in-the-blanks with your partner—you never know what goodies you'll uncover!

Conclusion

N ow that you've completed this collection of surveys, you hopefully have a better sense of your romantic self and a greater understanding of what will bring you fulfillment in your relationships. Now that you are armed with this valuable information, it is up to you to make use of your newfound self-knowledge and make the most of your love life. You probably saw patterns emerge in the way you handle particular situations, certain people and sensitive emotions. You can now step back and examine those patterns and the reasons behind them in order to ask yourself some hard questions: Are you happy with your current romantic behaviors? Are you attracting the right people? Are you an effective communicator? Can you make adjustments that will lead to more fulfilling experiences in the future? Are you ready and willing to change?

You can use the information gleaned in the surveys to develop a deeper understanding of both yourself and your approach to finding a mate. As we all know, the search for happiness and romantic satisfaction is an ever-evolving process whether you're looking for a partner, satisfied as a single or maintaining a long-term relationship. Regardless of your romantic status and relationship goals, these are issues that can always be addressed and there are improvements that can always be made.

In addition to offering you valuable information about yourself, we hope that you have enjoyed taking the surveys and learning how you handle a range of situations. Now that you have benefited from these surveys, you can have fun retaking the tests with friends or sharing them with your significant other. Additionally, previous survey takers have retaken the same questionnaires, either once a relationship has developed, once time has passed or once they have entered into a new relationship. We suggest coming back and retaking the surveys and comparing your results. You may be surprised to see significant differences in your responses the next time around.

Best of luck enjoying the surveys, getting to know yourself and finding true love and happiness.

About the Authors

Steve Klein, RateYourself Chairman

STEVE KLEIN is the CEO of ActiveBuddy, Inc., a software company based in New York City and Sunnyvale, California. Mr. Klein comes from a background in brand marketing and media planning and buying, and has leveraged that career experience to a pioneering role in numerous internet ventures. Mr. Klein founded iballs, an Internet media buying and data marketing company. He is a co-founder of Wit Dawntreader, a venture capital fund dedicated to early-stage Internet companies. His early career featured positions at numerous advertising agencies.

Amy Frome, Rate Yourself President

AMY FROME has media and consumer marketing background. Ms. Frome worked at ABC News's *Good Morning America* and *Barbara Walters Specials*. She then moved into advertising at Kirshenbaum, Bond & Partners, where she specialized in introducing new products. She has consulted for various Internet companies, and she is actively involved in numerous not-for-profit organizations, including AWARE, an organization dedicated to raising awareness and funds for women's causes. Ms. Frome graduated from Cornell University with a BA in Comparative Literature and holds an MBA from Columbia Business School.